Modern Critical Interpretations

Daniel Defoe's
Robinson Crusoe

Modern Critical Interpretations

These and other titles in preparation

Modern Critical Interpretations

Daniel Defoe's
Robinson Crusoe

Edited and with an introduction by

Harold Bloom
Sterling Professor of the Humanities
Yale University

Chelsea House Publishers ◊ *1988*

NEW YORK ◊ NEW HAVEN ◊ PHILADELPHIA

© 1988 by Chelsea House Publishers, a division
of Chelsea House Educational Communications, Inc.,
  95 Madison Avenue, New York, NY 10016
  345 Whitney Avenue, New Haven, CT 06511
  5068B West Chester Pike, Edgemont, PA 19028

Introduction © 1988 by Harold Bloom

Printed and bound in the United States of America

10 9 8 7 6 5 4 3 2 1.

∞ The paper used in this publication meets the minimum
requirements of the American National Standard for
Permanence of Paper for Printed Library Materials,
Z39.48–1984.

Library of Congress Cataloging-in-Publication Data
Daniel Defoe's Robinson Crusoe.
  (Modern critical interpretations)
  Bibliography: p.
  Includes index.
  Summary: A collection of seven critical essays on "Robinson
Crusoe" arranged in chronological order of their original
publication.
  1. Defoe, Daniel, 1661?–1731. Robinson Crusoe.
[1. Defoe, Daniel, 1661?–1731. Robinson Crusoe.
2. English literature—History and criticism]
I. Bloom, Harold. II. Series.
PR3403.Z5B55 1987   823'.5   87-11777
ISBN 0–87754–948–6 (alk. paper)

Contents

Editor's Note

This book brings together a representative selection of the best modern critical interpretations of Daniel Defoe's *Robinson Crusoe*. The critical essays are reprinted here in the chronological order of their original publication. I am grateful to Paul Kane for his assistance in editing this volume.

My introduction speculates upon the economic nature of Defoe's (and Crusoe's) God. The novelist Virginia Woolf, whose sensibility was so remote from Defoe's, begins the chronological sequence with her surprising appreciation of the "genius for fact" that is manifested in *Robinson Crusoe*.

Ian Watt, still our definitive historian of the rise of the novel, studies *Crusoe* as a great instance of Puritan individualism. The pattern of regeneration in Puritan spiritual autobiography is closely related to Crusoe's account of his experience in the essay of G. A. Starr.

J. Paul Hunter also reflects upon Puritan dialectics of salvation in regard to Crusoe's "retrospection and introspection." More aesthetic considerations are addressed by Leopold Damrosch, Jr., who judges *Robinson Crusoe* to be "a remarkable and unrepeatable reconciliation of myth with novel."

Michael Seidel, studying the interplay of the theme of exile and the narrative imagination, discovers in *Robinson Crusoe* the full representation of the exile as being sovereign, whether abroad or restored. In a grand coda to this volume, the distinguished Australian poet Alec Hope transfers the focus of our vision to Crusoe's man Friday, in a superb poem that is both its own source of value and a profound interpretation of Defoe's novel.

Introduction

I

Of his prayers and the like we take no account, since they are a source of
pleasure to him, and he looks upon them as so much recreation.

KARL MARX on *Robinson Crusoe*

I got so tired of the very colors!
One day I dyed a baby goat bright red
with my berries, just to see
something a little different.
And then his mother wouldn't recognize him.

ELIZABETH BISHOP, "Crusoe in England"

Had Karl Marx written *Robinson Crusoe,* it would have had even
more moral vigor, but at the expense of the image of freedom it still
provides for us. Had Elizabeth Bishop composed it, Defoe's narrative would have been enhanced as image and as impulse, but at the
expense of its Puritan plainness, its persuasive search for some evi-
dences of redemption. Certainly one of Defoe's novelistic virtues is
precisely what Ian Watt and Martin Price have emphasized it to be;
the puzzles of daily moral choice are omnipresent. Robinson Crusoe
and Moll Flanders are human—all-too-human—and suffer what
Calvin and Freud alike regarded as the economics of the spirit.

Defoe comes so early in the development of the modern novel
as a literary form that there is always a temptation to historicize
rather than to read him. But historicisms old and new are poor
substitutes for reading, and I do not find it useful to place *Robinson*
Crusoe and *Moll Flanders* in their contemporary context when I reread

1

them, as I have just done. Ian Watt usefully remarked: "Defoe's heroes . . . keep us more fully informed of their present stocks of money and commodities than any other characters in fiction." I suspect that this had more to do with Defoe than with his age, and that Defoe would have been no less obsessed with economic motives if he had written in the era of Queen Victoria. He was a hard man who had led a hard life: raised as a Dissenter in the London of the Great Plague and the Great Fire; enduring Newgate prison and the pillory in bankrupt middle age; working as a secret agent and a scandalous journalist until imprisoned again for debt and treason. Defoe died old, and so may be accounted as a survivor, but he had endured a good share of reality, and his novels reflect that endurance.

Dr. Johnson once said that only three books ought to have been still longer than they were: *Don Quixote, The Pilgrim's Progress,* and *Robinson Crusoe.* Defoe has authentic affinities with Bunyan, but there is nothing quixotic about Robinson Crusoe or Moll Flanders. All of Defoe's protagonists are pragmatic and prudent, because they have to be; there is no play in the world as they know it.

II

I did not read *Robinson Crusoe* as a child, and so missed an experience that continues to be all but universal; it remains a book that cannot fail with children. Yet, as Dickens observed, it is also "the only instance of an universally popular book that could make no one laugh and could make no one cry." Crusoe's singular tone, his self-baffled affect, does not bother children, who appear to empathize with a near-perfect solipsist who nevertheless exhibits energy and inventiveness throughout a quarter-century of solitude. Perhaps Crusoe's survival argues implicitly against every child's fear of dependency and prophesies the longed-for individuality that is still to come. Or perhaps every child's loneliness is answered in Crusoe's remarkable strength at sustaining solitude.

Though the identification of Defoe with Crusoe is never wholly overt, the reader senses its prevalence throughout the narrative. Defoe seems to me the least ironic of writers, and yet Crusoe's story is informed by an overwhelming irony. A restless wanderer, driven to travel and adventure by forces that he (and the reader) cannot comprehend, Crusoe is confined to an isolation that ought to madden him by turning him toward an unbearable inwardness. Yet his sanity prevails, despite his apparent imprisonment. Defoe had borne much; Newgate and the pillory were nightmare experiences. Crusoe bears more, yet Defoe will not describe his hero's suffering as being psychic. As Virginia Woolf noted, Defoe "takes the opposite way from the psychologist's—he describes the effect of emotion on the body, not on the mind." Nowhere is this stronger than in Crusoe's agony as he views a shipwreck:

> Such certainly was the Case of these Men, of whom I could not so much as see room to suppose any of them were sav'd; nothing could make it rational, so much as to wish, or expect that they did not all perish there; except the Possibility only of their being taken up by another Ship in Company, and this was but meer Possibility indeed; for I saw not the least Signal or Appearance of any such Thing.
>
> I cannot explain by any possible Energy of Words what a strange longing or hankering of Desires I felt in my Soul upon this Sight; breaking out sometimes thus; O that there had been but one or two; nay, or but one Soul sav'd out of this Ship, to have escap'd to me, that I might but have had one Companion, one Fellow-Creature to have spoken to me, and to have convers'd with! In all the Time of my solitary Life, I never felt so earnest, so strong a Desire after the Society of my Fellow-Creatures, or so deep a Regret at the want of it.
>
> There are some secret moving Springs in the Affections, which when they are set a going by some Object in view; or be it some Object, though not in view, yet rendred present to the Mind by the Power of Imagination, that Motion carries out the Soul by its Impetuosity to such violent eager embracings of the Object, that the Absence of it is unsupportable.
>
> Such were these earnest Wishings, That but one Man had been sav'd! *O that it had been but One!* I believe I repeated the Words, *O that it had been but One!* a thousand Times; and the Desires were so mov'd by it, that when I spoke the Words, my Hands would clinch together, and my Fingers press the Palms of my Hands, that if I had had any soft Thing in my Hand, it would have crusht it involuntarily; and my Teeth in my Head wou'd strike together,

and set against one another so strong, that for some time
I cou'd not part them again.

These are the reactions of a compulsive craftsman who has found his freedom but cannot bear its full sublimity. Crusoe, himself the least sublime of personages, is embedded throughout in a sublime situation, best epitomized by the ghastly cannibal feasts he spies upon, and from which he rescues his man Friday. Against his superior technology and Puritan resolve, the cannibals offer almost no resistance, so that the rapid conversion of the cannibal Friday to Protestant theology and diet is not unconvincing. What may baffle the average rereader is Crusoe's comparative dearth of Protestant inwardness. It is not that Marx was accurate and that Crusoe becomes Protestant only upon the Sabbath, but rather that Defoe's God is himself a technocrat and an individualist, not much given to the nicer emotions.

Defoe's God can be visualized as a giant tradesman, coping with the universe as Crusoe makes do on his island, but with teeming millions of adoring Fridays where Crusoe enjoys the devotion of just one.

Robinson Crusoe

Virginia Woolf

There are many ways of approaching this classical volume; but which shall we choose? Shall we begin by saying that, since Sidney died at Zutphen leaving the *Arcadia* unfinished, great changes had come over English life, and the novel had chosen, or had been forced to choose, its direction? A middle class had come into existence, able to read and anxious to read not only about the loves of princes and princesses, but about themselves and the details of their humdrum lives. Stretched upon a thousand pens, prose had accommodated itself to the demand; it had fitted itself to express the facts of life rather than the poetry. That is certainly one way of approaching *Robinson Crusoe*—through the development of the novel; but another immediately suggests itself—through the life of the author. Here too, in the heavenly pastures of biography, we may spend many more hours than are needed to read the book itself from cover to cover. The date of Defoe's birth, to begin with, is doubtful—was it 1660 or 1661? Then again, did he spell his name in one word or in two? And who were his ancestors? He is said to have been a hosier; but what, after all, was a hosier in the seventeenth century? He became a pamphleteer, and enjoyed the confidence of William the Third; one of his pamphlets caused him to be stood in the pillory and imprisoned at Newgate; he was employed by Harley and later by Godolphin; he was the first of the hireling journalists; he wrote innumerable pamphlets and articles; also *Moll Flanders* and *Robinson Crusoe;* he had a wife and six children; was spare in figure, with a hooked nose, a

From *Collected Essays: Volume One*. © 1966 by Leonard Woolf. Hogarth Press, 1966.

sharp chin, grey eyes, and a large mole near his mouth. Nobody who has any slight acquaintance with English literature needs to be told how many hours can be spent and how many lives have been spent in tracing the development of the novel and in examining the chins of the novelists. Only now and then, as we turn from theory to biography and from biography to theory, a doubt insinuates itself— if we knew the very moment of Defoe's birth and whom he loved and why, if we had by heart the history of the origin, rise, growth, decline, and fall of the English novel from its conception (say) in Egypt to its decease in the wilds (perhaps) of Paraguay, should we suck an ounce of additional pleasure from *Robinson Crusoe* or read it one whit more intelligently?

For the book itself remains. However we may wind and wriggle, loiter and dally in our approach to books, a lonely battle waits us at the end. There is a piece of business to be transacted between writer and reader before any further dealings are possible, and to be reminded in the middle of this private interview that Defoe sold stockings, had brown hair, and was stood in the pillory is a distraction and a worry. Our first task, and it is often formidable enough, is to master his perspective. Until we know how the novelist orders his world, the ornaments of that world, which the critics press upon us, the adventures of the writer, to which biographers draw attention, are superfluous possessions of which we can make no use. All alone we must climb upon the novelist's shoulders and gaze through his eyes until we, too, understand in what order he ranges the large common objects upon which novelists are fated to gaze: man and men; behind them Nature; and above them that power which for convenience and brevity we may call God. And at once confusion, misjudgement, and difficulty begin. Simple as they appear to us, these objects can be made monstrous and indeed unrecognizable by the manner in which the novelist relates them to each other. It would seem to be true that people who live cheek by jowl and breathe the same air vary enormously in their sense of proportion; to one the human being is vast, the tree minute; to the other, trees are huge and human beings insignificant little objects in the background. So, in spite of the text-books, writers may live at the same time and see nothing the same size. Here is Scott, for example, with his mountains looming huge and his men therefore drawn to scale; Jane Austen picking out the roses on her tea-cups to match the wit of her dialogues; while Peacock bends over heaven and earth one fantastic distorting mirror in which a tea-cup may be Vesuvius or Vesuvius a tea-cup. Nevertheless Scott, Jane Austen, and Peacock lived through the same years; they saw the same world; they are covered in the textbooks by the same stretch of literary history. It is in their perspective that they are different. If, then, it were granted us to grasp this firmly, for ourselves, the battle would end in victory; and we could turn, secure in our intimacy, to enjoy the various delights with which the critics and biographers so generously supply us.

But here many difficulties arise. For we have our own vision of the world; we have made it from our own experience and prejudices, and it is therefore bound up with our own vanities and loves. It is impossible not to feel injured and insulted if tricks are played and our private harmony is upset. Thus when *Jude the Obscure* appears or a new volume of Proust, the newspapers are flooded with protests. Major Gibbs of Cheltenhem would put a bullet through his head tomorrow if life were as Hardy paints it; Miss Wiggs of Hampstead must protest that though Proust's art is wonderful, the real world, she thanks God, has nothing in common with the distortions of a perverted Frenchman. Both the gentleman and the lady are trying to control the novelist's perspective so that it shall resemble and reinforce their own. But the great writer—the Hardy or the Proust—goes on his way regardless of the rights of private property; by the sweat of his brow he brings order from chaos; he plants his tree there, and his man here; he makes the figure of his deity remote or present as he wills. In masterpieces—books, that is, where the vision is clear and order has been achieved—he inflicts his own perspective upon us so severely that as often as not we suffer agonies—our vanity is injured because our own order is upset; we are afraid because the old supports are being wrenched from us; and we are bored—for what pleasure or amusement can be plucked from a brand new idea? Yet from anger, fear, and boredom a rare and lasting delight is sometimes born.

Robinson Crusoe, it may be, is a case in point. It is a masterpiece, and it is a masterpiece largely because Defoe has throughout kept consistently to his own sense of perspective. For this reason he thwarts us and flouts us at every turn. Let us look at the theme largely and loosely, comparing it with our preconceptions. It is, we know, the story of a man who is thrown, after many perils and adventures, alone upon a desert island. The mere suggestion—peril and solitude and a desert island—is enough to rouse in us the expectation of some far land on the limits of the world; of the sun rising and the sun setting; of man, isolated from his kind, brooding alone upon the nature of society and the strange ways of men. Before we open the book we have perhaps vaguely sketched out the kind of pleasure we expect it to give us. We read; and we are rudely contradicted on every page. There are no sunsets and no sunrises; there is no solitude and no soul. There is, on the contrary, staring us full in the face nothing but a large earthenware pot. We are told, that is to say, that it was the first of September, 1651; that the hero's name is Robinson Crusoe; and that his father has the gout. Obviously, then, we must alter our attitude. Reality, fact, substance is going to dominate all that follows. We must hastily alter out proportions throughout; Nature must furl her splendid purples; she is only the giver of drought and water; man must be reduced to a struggling, life-preserving animal; and God shrivel into a magistrate whose seat, substantial and somewhat hard, is only a little way above the horizon. Each sortie of ours in pursuit of information upon these cardinal points of perspective—God, man, Nature—is snubbed back with ruthless common sense. Robinson Crusoe thinks of God: "sometimes I would expostulate with myself, why providence should thus completely ruin its creatures. . . . But something always return'd swift upon me to check these thoughts." God does not exist. He thinks of Nature, the fields "adorn'd with flowers and grass, and full of very fine woods," but the important thing about a wood is that it harbours an abundance of parrots who may be tamed and taught to speak. Nature does not exist. He considers the dead, whom he has killed himself. It is of the utmost importance that they should be buried at once, for "they lay open to the sun and would presently be offensive." Death does not exist. Nothing exists except an earthenware pot. Finally, that is to say, we are forced to drop our own preconceptions and to accept what Defoe himself wishes to give us.

Let us then go back to the beginning and repeat again, "I was born in the year 1632 in the city of York of a good family." Nothing could be plainer, more matter of fact, than that beginning. We are drawn on soberly to consider all the blessings of orderly, industrious middle-class life. There is no greater good fortune we are assured than to be born of the British middle class. The great are to be pitied and so are the poor; both are exposed to distempers and uneasiness; the middle station between the mean and the great is the best; and its virtues—temperance, moderation, quietness, and health—are the most desirable. It was a sorry thing, then, when by some evil fate a middle-class youth was bitten with the foolish love of adventure. So he proses on, drawing, little by little, his own portrait, so that we never forget it—imprinting upon us indelibly, for he never forgets it either, his shrewdness, his caution, his love of order and comfort and respectability; until by whatever means, we find ourselves at sea, in a storm; and, peering out, everything is seen precisely as it appears to Robinson Crusoe. The waves, the seamen, the sky, the ship—all are seen through those shrewd, middle-class, unimaginative eyes. There is no escaping him. Everything appears as it would appear to that naturally cautious, apprehensive, conventional, and solidly matter-of-fact intelligence. He is incapable of enthusiasm. He has a natural slight distaste for the sublimities of Nature. He suspects even Providence of exaggeration. He is so busy and has such an eye to the main chance that he notices only a tenth part of what is going on round him. Everything is capable of a rational explanation, he is sure, if only he had time to attend to it. We are much more alarmed by the "vast great creatures" that swim out in the night and surround his boat than he is. He at once takes his gun and fires at them, and off they swim—whether they are lions or not he really cannot say. Thus before we know it we are opening our mouths wider and wider. We are swallowing monsters that we should have jibbed at if they had been offered us by an imaginative and flamboyant traveller. But anything that this sturdy middle-class man notices can be taken for a fact. He is forever counting his barrels, and making sensible provisions for his water supply; nor do we ever find him tripping even in a matter of detail. Has he forgotten, we wonder, that he has a great lump of beeswax on board? Not at all. But as he had already made candles out of it, it is not nearly as great on page thirty-eight as it was on page twenty-three. When for a wonder he leaves some inconsistency hanging loose—why if the wild cats are so very tame are the goats so very shy?—we are not seriously perturbed, for we are sure that there was a reason, and a very good one, had he time to give it us. But the pressure of life when one is fending entirely for oneself alone on a desert island is really no laughing matter. It is no crying one either. A man must have an eye to everything; it is no time for raptures about Nature when the lightning may explode one's gunpowder—it is imperative to seek a safer lodging for it. And so by means of telling the truth undeviatingly as it appears to him—by being a great artist and forgoing this and daring that in order to give effect to his prime quality, a sense of reality—he comes in the end to make common actions dignified and common objects beautiful. To dig, to bake, to plant, to build—how serious these simple occupations are; hatchets, scissors, logs, axes—how beautiful these simple objects become. Unimpeded by comment, the story marches on with magnificent downright simplicity. Yet how could comment have made it more impressive? It is true that he takes the opposite way from the psychologist's—he describes the effect of emotion on the body, not on the mind. But when he says how, in a moment of anguish, he clinched his hands so that any soft thing would have been crushed; how "my teeth in my head would strike together, and set against one another so strong that for the time I could not part them again," the effect is as deep as pages of analysis could have made it. His own instinct in the matter is right. "Let the naturalists," he says, "explain these things, and the reason and manner of them; all I can say to them is, to describe the fact. . . ." If you are Defoe, certainly to describe the fact is enough; for the fact is the right fact. By means of this genius for fact Defoe achieves effects that are beyond any but the great masters of descriptive prose. He has only to say a word or two about "the grey of the morning" to paint vividly a windy dawn. A sense of desolation and of the deaths of many men is conveyed by remarking in the most prosaic way in the world, "I never saw them afterwards, or any sign of them except three of their hats, one cap, and two shoes that were not fellows." When at last he exclaims, "Then to see how like a king I din'd too all alone, attended by my servants"—his parrot and his dog and his two cats, we cannot help but feel that all humanity is on a desert island alone—though Defoe at once informs us, for he has a way of snubbing off our enthusiasms, that the cats were not the same cats that had come in the ship. Both of those were dead; these cats were new cats, and as a matter of fact cats became very troublesome before long from their fecundity, whereas dogs, oddly enough, did not breed at all.

Thus Defoe, by reiterating that nothing but a plain earthenware pot stands in the foreground, persuades us to see remote islands and the solitudes of the human soul. By believing fixedly in the solidity of the pot and its earthiness, he has subdued every other element to his design; he has roped the whole universe into harmony. And is there any reason, we ask as we shut the book, why the perspective that a plain earthenware pot exacts should not satisfy us as completely, once we grasp it, as man himself in all his sublimity standing against a background of broken mountains and tumbling oceans with stars flaming in the sky?

Individualism and the Novel

Ian Watt

The novel's serious concern with the daily lives of ordinary people
seems to depend upon two important general conditions: the society
must value every individual highly enough to consider him the proper
subject of its serious literature; and there must be enough variety of
belief and action among ordinary people for a detailed account of
them to be of interest to other ordinary people, the readers of novels.
It is probable that neither of these conditions for the existence of the
novel obtained very widely until fairly recently, because they both
depend on the rise of a society characterised by that vast complex of
interdependent factors denoted by the term "individualism."

Even the word is recent, dating only from the middle of the
nineteenth century. In all ages, no doubt, and in all societies, some
people have been "individualists" in the sense that they were egocentric, unique or conspicuously independent of current opinions
and habits; but the concept of individualism involves much more
than this. It posits a whole society mainly governed by the idea of
every individual's intrinsic independence both from other individuals
and from that multifarious allegiance to past modes of thought and
action denoted by the word "tradition"—a force that is always social, not individual. The existence of such a society, in turn, obviously depends on a special type of economic and political organisation
and on an appropriate ideology; more specifically, on an economic

From *The Rise of the Novel: Studies in Defoe, Richardson and Fielding.* © 1957 by Ian
Watt. Chatto & Windus, 1957.

and political organisation which allows its members a very wide range of choices in their actions, and on an ideology primarily based, not on the tradition of the past, but on the autonomy of the individual, irrespective of his particular social status or personal capacity. It is generally agreed that modern society is uniquely individualist in these respects, and that of the many historical causes for its emergence two are of supreme importance—the rise of modern industrial capitalism and the spread of Protestantism, especially in its Calvinist or Puritan forms.

I

Capitalism brought a great increase of economic specialisation; and this, combined with a less rigid and homogeneous social structure, and a less absolutist and more democratic political system, enormously increased the individual's freedom of choice. For those fully exposed to the new economic order, the effective entity on which social arrangements were now based was no longer the family, nor the church, nor the guild, nor the township, nor any other collective unit, but the individual: he alone was primarily responsible for determining his own economic, social, political and religious roles.

It is very difficult to say when this change of orientation began to affect society as a whole—probably not until the nineteenth century. But the movement certainly began much earlier. In the sixteenth century the Reformation and the rise of national states decisively challenged the substantial social homogeneity of mediaeval Christendom, and, in the famous words of Maitland, "for the first time, the Absolute State faced the Absolute Individual." Outside the political and religious sphere, however, change was slow, and it is likely that it was not until the further development of industrial capitalism, especially in England and in the Low Countries, that a mainly individualist social and economic structure came into being and started to affect a considerable part, although by no means a majority, of the total population.

It is, at least, generally agreed that the foundations of the new order were laid in the period immediately following the Glorious Revolution of 1689. The commercial and industrial classes, who were the prime agents in bringing about the individualist social order, had achieved greater political and economic power; and this power was already being reflected in the domain of literature. The middle classes of the towns, we have seen, were becoming much more important in the reading public; and at the same time literature begin to view trade, commerce and industry with favour. This was a rather new development. Earlier writers, Spenser, Shakespeare, Donne, Ben Jonson and Dryden, for example, had tended to support the traditional economic and social order and had attacked many of the symptoms of emergent individualism. By the beginning of the eighteenth century, however, Addison, Steele and Defoe were somewhat ostentatiously setting the seal of literary approval on the heroes of economic individualism.

The new orientation was equally evident in the philosophical domain. The great English empiricists of the seventeenth century were as vigorously individualist in their political and ethical thought as in their epistemology. Bacon hoped to make a really new start in social theory by applying his inductive method to an accumulation of factual data about a great number of particular individuals; Hobbes, also feeling that he was dealing with a subject that had not been properly approached before, based his political and ethical theory on the fundamentally egocentric psychological constitution of the individual; while in his *Two Treatises of Government* (1690) Lock constructed the class system of political thought based on the indefeasibility of individual rights, as against the more traditional ones of Church, Family or King. That these thinkers should have been the political and psychological vanguard of nascent individualism, as well as the pioneers of its theory of knowledge, suggests how closely linked their reorientations were both in themselves and in relation to the innovations of the novel. For, just as there is a basic congruity between the non-realist nature of the literary forms of the Greeks, their intensely social, or civic, moral outlook, and their philosophical preference for the universal, so the modern novel is closely allied on the one hand to the realist epistemology of the modern period, and on the other to the individualism of its social structure. In the literary, the philosophical and the social spheres alike the classical focus on the ideal, the universal and the corporate has shifted completely, and the modern field of vision is mainly occupied by the discrete particular, the directly apprehended sensum, and the autonomous individual.

Defoe, whose philosophical outlook has much in common with that of the English empiricists of the seventeenth century, expressed the diverse elements of individualism more completely than any previous writer, and his work offers a unique demonstration of the connection between individualism in its many forms and the rise of the novel. This connection is shown particularly clearly and comprehensively in his first novel, *Robinson Crusoe*.

II

(a)

Robinson Crusoe has been very appropriately used by many economic theorists as their illustration of *homo economicus*. Just as "the body politic" was the symbol of the communal way of thought typical of previous societies, so "economic man" symbolised the new outlook of individualism in its economic aspect. Adam Smith has been charged with the invention; actually, the concept is much older, but it is natural that it should have come to the fore as an abstraction expressing the individualism of the economic system as a whole only when the individualism of that system itself had reached an advanced stage of development.

That Robinson Crusoe, like Defoe's other main characters, Moll Flanders, Roxana, Colonel Jacque and Captain Singleton, is an embodiment of economic individualism hardly needs demonstration. All Defoe's heroes pursue money, which he characteristically called "the general denominating article in the world," and they pursue it very methodically according to the profit and loss bookkeeping which Max Weber considered to be the distinctive technical feature of modern capitalism. Defoe's heroes, we observe, have no need to learn this technique; whatever the circumstances of their birth and education, they have it in their blood, and keep us more fully informed of their present stocks of money and commodities than any other characters in fiction. Crusoe's bookkeeping conscience, indeed, has established an effective priority over his other thoughts and emotions; when his Lisbon steward offers him 160 moidores to alleviate his momentary difficulties on return, Crusoe relates: "I could hardly refrain from tears while he spoke; in short, I took 100 of the moidores, and called for a pen and ink to give him a receipt for them."

Bookkeeping is but one aspect of a central theme in the modern social order. Our civilisation as a whole is based on individual contractual relationships, as opposed to the unwritten, traditional and collective relationships of previous societies; and the idea of contract played an important part in the theoretical development of political individualism. It had featured prominently in the fight against the Stuarts, and it was enshrined in Locke's political system. Locke, indeed, thought that contractual relationships were binding even in the state of nature; Crusoe, we notice, acts like a good Lockean—when others arrive on the island he forces them to accept his dominion with written contracts acknowledging his absolute power (even though we have previously been told that he has run out of ink).

But the primacy of the economic motive, and an innate reverence for bookkeeping and the law of contract are by no means the only matters in which Robinson Crusoe is a symbol of the processes associated with the rise of economic individualism. The hypostasis of the economic motive logically entails a devaluation of other modes of thought, feeling and action: the various forms of traditional group relationship, the family, the guild, the village, the sense of nationality—all are weakened, and so, too, are the competing claims of non-economic individual achievement and enjoyment, ranging from spiritual salvation to the pleasures of recreation.

This inclusive reordering of the components of human society tends to occur wherever industrial capitalism becomes the dominant force in the economic structure, and it naturally became evident particularly early in England. By the middle of the eighteenth century, indeed, it had already become something of a commonplace. Goldsmith, for instance, thus described the concomitants of England's vaunted freedom in *The Traveller* (1764):

> That independence Britons prize too high,
> Keeps man from man, and breaks the social tie;
> The self-dependent lordlings stand alone,
> All claims that bind and sweeten life unknown;
> Here by the bonds of nature feebly held,
> Minds combat minds, repelling and repell'd . . .
>   Nor this the worst. As nature's ties decay,
> As duty, love, and honour fail to sway,
> Fictitious bonds, the bonds of wealth and law,
> Still gather strength, and force unwilling awe.

Unlike Goldsmith, Defoe was not a professed enemy of the new order—quite the reverse; nevertheless there is much in *Robinson Crusoe* that bears out Goldsmith's picture, as can be seen in Defoe's treatment of such group relationships as the family or the nation.

For the most part, Defoe's heroes either have no family, like Moll Flanders, Colonel Jacque and Captain Singleton, or leave it at an early age never to return, like Roxana and Robinson Crusoe. Not too much importance can be attached to this fact, since adventure stories demand the absence of conventional social ties. Still, in *Robinson Crusoe* at least, the hero has a home and family, and leaves them for the classic reason of homo economicus—that it is necessary to better his economic condition. "Something fatal in that propension of nature" calls him to the sea and adventure, and against "settling to business"; in the station to which he is born—"the upper station of low life"; and this despite the panegyric which his father makes of that condition. Later he sees this lack of "confined desires," this dissatisfaction with "the state wherein God and Nature has placed" him, as his "original sin." At the time, however, the argument between his parents and himself is a debate, not about filial duty or religion, but about whether going or staying is likely to be the most advantageous course materially: both sides accept the economic argument as primary. And, of course, Crusoe actually gains by his "original sin," and becomes richer than his father was.

Crusoe's "original sin" is really the dynamic tendency of capitalism itself, whose aim is never merely to maintain the status quo, but to transform it incessantly. Leaving home, improving on the lot one was born to, is a vital feature of the individualist pattern of life. It may be regarded as the economic and social embodiment of the "uneasiness" which Locke had made the centre of his system of motivation, an uneasiness whose existence was, in the very opposite outlook of Pascal, the index of the enduring misery of mortal man. "All the unhappiness of men arises from one single fact, that they cannot stay quietly in their own room" Pascal had written. Defoe's hero is far from agreeing. Even when he is old, Crusoe tells us how: "nothing else offering, and finding that really stirring about and trading, the profit being so great, and, as I may say, certain, had more pleasure in it, and more satisfaction to the mind, than sitting still, which, to me especially, was the unhappiest part of life." So, in the *Farther Adventures,* Crusoe sets out on yet another lucrative Odyssey.

The fundamental tendency of economic individualism, then, prevents Crusoe from paying much heed to the ties of family, whether as a son or a husband. This is in direct contradiction to the great stress which Defoe lays on the social and religious importance of the family in his didactic works such as the *Family Instructor;* but his novels reflect not theory but practice, and they accord these ties a very minor, and on the whole obstructive, role.

Rational scrutiny of one's own economic interest may lead one to be as little bound by national as by family ties. Defoe certainly valued individuals and countries alike primarily on their economic merits. Thus one of his most patriotic utterances takes the characteristic form of claiming that his compatriots have a greater productive output per hour than the workmen of any other country. Crusoe, we notice, whom Walter de la Mare has just called Defoe's Elective Affinity, shows xenophobia mainly where the economic virtues are absent. When they are present—as in the Spanish Governor, a French papist priest, a faithful Portuguese factor—his praise is unstinted. On the other hand, he condemns many Englishmen, such as his English settlers on the island, for their lack of industry. Crusoe, one feels, is not bound to his country by sentimental ties, any more than to his family; he is satisfied by people, whatever their nationality, who are good to do business with; and he feels, like Moll Flanders, that "with money in the pocket one is at home anywhere."

What might at first appear to place *Robinson Crusoe* in the somewhat special category of "Travel and Adventure" does not, then, altogether do so. The plot's reliance on travel does tend to allot *Robinson Crusoe* a somewhat peripheral position in the novel's line of development, since it removes the hero from his usual setting in a stable and cohesive pattern of social relations. But Crusoe is not a mere footloose adventurer, and his travels, like his freedom from social ties, are merely somewhat extreme cases of tendencies that are normal in modern society as a whole, since, by making the pursuit of gain a primary motive, economic individualism has much increased the mobility of the individual. More specifically, Robinson Crusoe's career is based, as modern scholarship has shown, on some of the innumerable volumes which recounted the exploits of those voyagers who had done so much in the sixteenth century to assist the development of capitalism by providing the gold, slaves and tropical products on which trade expansion depended; and who had continued the process in the seventeenth century by developing the colonies and world markets on which the future progress of capitalism depended.

Defoe's plot, then, expresses some of the most important tendencies of the life of his time, and it is this which sets his hero apart from most of the travellers in literature. Robinson Crusoe is not, like Autolycus, a commercial traveller rooted in an extended but still familiar locality; nor is he, like Ulysses, an unwilling voyager trying to get back to his family and his native land: profit is Crusoe's only vocation, and the whole world is his territory.

The primacy of individual economic advantage has tended to diminish the importance of personal as well as group relationships, and especially of those based on sex; for sex, as Weber pointed out, being one of the strongest non-rational factors in human life, is one of the strongest potential menaces to the individual's rational pursuit of economic ends, and it has therefore, as we shall see, been placed under particularly strong controls in the ideology of industrial capitalism.

Romantic love has certainly had no greater antagonist among the novelists than Defoe. Even sexual satisfaction—where he speaks of it—tends to be minimised; he protested in *The Review,* for example, that "the Trifle called Pleasure in it" was "not worth the Repentance." As to marriage, his attitude is complicated by the fact that economic and moral virtue in the male is no guarantee of a profitable matrimonial investment: on his colony "as it often happens in the world (what the wise ends of God's Providence are in such a disposition of things I cannot say), the two honest fellows had the two worst wives, and the three reprobates, that were scarce worth hanging . . . had three clever, diligent, careful and ingenious wives." His puzzled parenthesis bears eloquent testimony to the seriousness with which he views this flaw in the rationality of Providence.

It is not surprising, therefore, that love plays little part in Crusoe's own life, and that even the temptations of sex are excluded from the scene of his greatest triumphs, the island. When Crusoe does notice the lack of "society" there, he prays for the solace of company, but we observe that what he desires is a male slave. Then, with Friday, he enjoys an idyll without benefit of woman—a revolutionary departure from the traditional expectations aroused by desert islands from the *Odyssey* to the *New Yorker*.

When eventually Crusoe returns to civilisation, sex is still strictly subordinated to business. Only when his financial position has been fully secured by a further voyage does he marry; and all he tells us of this supreme human adventure is that it was "not either to my disadvantage or dissatisfaction." This, the birth of three children, and his wife's death, however, comprise only the early part of a sentence, which ends with plans for a further voyage.

Women have only one important role to play, and that is economic. When Crusoe's colonists draw lots for five women, we are gleefully informed that:

> He that drew to choose first . . . took her that was reckoned the homeliest and eldest of the five, which made mirth enough among the rest . . . but the fellow considered better than any of them, that it was application and business that they were to expect assistance in as much as anything else; and she proved the best wife of all the parcel.

"The best wife of all the parcel." The language of commerce here reminds us that Dickens once decided on the basis of Defoe's treatment of women that he must have been "a precious dry and disagreeable article himself."

The same devaluation of non-economic factors can be seen in Crusoe's other personal relationships. He treats them all in terms of their commodity value. The clearest case is that of Xury, the Moorish boy who helped him to escape from slavery and on another occasion offered to prove his devotion by sacrificing his own life. Crusoe very properly resolves "to love him ever after" and promises "to make him a great man." But when chance leads them to the Portuguese Captain, who offers Crusoe sixty pieces of eight—twice Judas's figure—he cannot resist the bargain, and sells Xury into slavery. He has momentary scruples, it is true, but they are cheaply satisfied by securing a promise from the new owner to "set him free in ten years if he turn Christian." Remorse later supervenes, but only when the tasks of his island life make manpower more valuable to him than money.

Crusoe's relations with Man Friday are similarly egocentric. He does not ask him his name, but gives him one. Even in language—

the medium whereby human beings may achieve something more than animal relationships with each other, as Crusoe himself wrote in his *Serious Reflections*—Crusoe is a strict utilitarian. "I likewise taught him to say Yes and No," he tells us; but Friday still speaks pidgin English at the end of their long association, as Defoe's contemporary critic Charles Gildon pointed out.

Yet Crusoe regards the relationship as ideal. He is "as perfectly and completely happy if any such thing as complete happiness can be found in a sublunary state." A functional silence, broken only by an occasional "No, Friday," or an abject "Yes, Master," is the golden music of Crusoe's *île joyeuse*. It seems that man's social nature, his need for friendship and understanding, is wholly satisfied by the righteous bestowal or grateful receipt, of benevolent but not undemanding patronage. It is true that later, as with Xury, Crusoe promises himself "to do something considerable" for his servant, "if he outlive me." Fortunately, no such sacrifice is called for, as Friday dies at sea, to be rewarded only by a brief word of obituary compassion.

Emotional ties, then, and personal relationships generally, play a very minor part in *Robinson Crusoe,* except when they are focussed on economic matters. For instance, after Crusoe has left, it is only when his faithful old agent in Lisbon reveals that he is now a very rich man that we get any emotional climax: "I turned pale and grew sick; and had not the old man run and fetched me a cordial, I believe the sudden surprise of joy had overset nature, and I had died upon the spot." Only money—fortune in its modern sense—is a proper cause of deep feeling; and friendship is accorded only to those who can safely be entrusted with Crusoe's economic interests.

Sitting still, we saw, was "the unhappiest part of life" to Robinson Crusoe; leisure pursuits are almost as bad. In this he resembles his author, who seems to have made as few concessions to such distractions as anyone. The fewness of Defoe's literary friendships has been commented on, and he is perhaps a unique example of a great writer who was very little interested in literature, and says nothing of interest about it as literature.

In his blindness to aesthetic experience Crusoe is Defoe's peer. We can say of him as Marx said of his archetypal capitalist: "enjoyment is subordinated to capital, and the individual who enjoys to the individual who capitalises." Some of the French versions of *Robinson Crusoe* makes him address hymns of praise to nature, beginning "Oh

Nature!" Defoe did not. The natural scene on the island appeals not for adoration, but for exploitation; wherever Crusoe looks his acres cry out so loud for improvement that he has no leisure to observe that they also compose a landscape.

Of course, in a wintry way, Crusoe has his pleasures. If he does not, like Selkirk, dance with his goats, he at least plays with them, and with his parrot and his cats; but his deepest satisfactions come from surveying his stock of goods: "I had everything so ready at my hand," he says, "that it was a great pleasure to me to see all my goods in such order, and especially to find my stock of all necessaries so great."

(b)

If Robinson Crusoe's character depends very largely on the psychological and social orientations of economic individualism, the appeal of his adventures to the reader seems mainly to derive from the effects of another important concomitant of modern capitalism, economic specialisation.

The division of labour has done much to make the novel possible: partly because the more specialised the social and economic structure, the greater the number of significant differences of character, attitude and experience in contemporary life which the novelist can portray, and which are of interest to his readers; partly because, by increasing the amount of leisure, economic specialisation provides the kind of mass audience with which the novel is associated; and partly because this specialisation creates particular needs in that audience which the novel satisfies. Such, at least, was the general view of T. H. Green: "In the progressive division of labour, while we become more useful as citizens, we seem to lose our completeness as men . . . the perfect organisation of modern society removes the excitement of adventure and the occasion for independent effort. There is less of human interest to touch us within our calling." "The alleviation" of this situation, Green concluded, "is to be found in the newspaper and the novel."

It is very likely that the lack of variety and stimulation in the daily task as a result of economic specialisation is largely responsible for the unique dependence of the individual in our culture upon the substitute experiences provided by the printing press, particularly in the forms of journalism and the novel. *Robinson Crusoe,* however, is a much more direct illustration of Green's thesis, since much of its appeal obviously depends on the quality of the "occasions for independent effort" in the economic realm which it offers Defoe's hero, efforts which the reader can share vicariously. The appeal of these efforts is surely a measure of the depth of the deprivations involved by economic specialisation, deprivations whose far-reaching nature is suggested by the way our civilisation has reintroduced some of the basic economic processes as therapeutic recreations: in gardening, home-weaving, pottery, camping, woodwork and keeping pets, we can all participate in the character-forming satisfactions which circumstances force on Defoe's hero; and like him, demonstrate what we would not otherwise know, that "by making the most rational judgement of things, every man may be in time master of every mechanic art."

Defoe was certainly aware of how the increasing economic specialisation which was a feature of the life of his time had made most of the "mechanic arts" alien to the experience of his readers. When Crusoe makes bread, for instance, he reflects that " 'Tis a little wonderful and what I believe few people have thought much upon, viz., the strange multitude of little things necessary in the providing, procuring, curing, dressing, making and finishing this one article of bread." Defoe's description goes on for seven pages, pages that would have been of little interest to people in mediaeval or Tudor society, who saw this and other basic economic processes going on daily in their own households. But by the early eighteenth century, as Kalm reported, most women did not "bake, because there is a baker in every parish or village," and Defoe could therefore expect his readers to be interested in the very detailed descriptions of the economic life which comprise such an important and memorable part of his narrative.

Robinson Crusoe, of course, does not deal with the actual economic life of Defoe's own time and place. It would be somewhat contrary to the facts of economic life under the division of labour to show the average individual's manual labour as interesting or inspiring; to take Adam Smith's famous example of the division of labour in *The Wealth of Nations,* the man who performs one of the many separate operations in the manufacture of a pin is unlikely to find his task as absorbing and interesting as Crusoe does. So Defoe sets back the economic clock, and takes his hero to a primitive environment, where labour can be presented as varied and inspiring, and where it has the further significant difference from the pin-maker's at home that there is an absolute equivalence between individual effort and individual reward. This was the final change from contemporary economic conditions which was necessary to enable Defoe to give narrative expression to the ideological counterpart of the Division of Labour, the Dignity of Labour.

The creed of the dignity of labour is not wholly modern: in classical times the Cynics and Stoics had opposed the denigration of manual labour which is a necessary part of a slave-owning society's scale of values; and later, Christianity, originally associated mainly with slaves and the poor, had done much to remove the odium on manual labour. The idea, however, was only fully developed in the modern period, presumably because its compensatory affirmation became the more necessary as the development of economic specialisation made manual labour more stultifying; and the creed itself is closely associated with the advent of Protestantism. Calvinism in particular tended to make its adherents forget the idea that labour was God's punishment for Adam's disobedience, by emphasising the very different idea that untiring stewardship of the material gifts of God was a paramount religious and ethical obligation.

The quality of Crusoe's stewardship cannot be doubted; he allows himself little time for rest, and even the advent of new manpower—Friday's—is a signal, not for relaxation, but for expanded production. Defoe clearly belongs to the tradition of Ascetic Protestantism. He had written much that sounds like the formulations of Weber, Troeltsch and Tawney; in Dickory Cronke's aphorism, for example: "When you find yourself sleepy in a morning, rouse yourself, and consider that you are born to business, and that in doing good in your generation, you answer your character and act like a man." He had even—with a certain sophistic obtuseness—propounded the view that the pursuit of economic utility was quite literally an imitation of Christ: "Usefulness being the great pleasure, and justly deem'd by all good men the truest and noblest end of life, in which men come nearest to the character of our B. Saviour, who went about doing good."

Defoe's attitude here exhibits a confusion of religious and material values to which the Puritan gospel of the dignity of labour was peculiarly liable: once the highest spiritual values had been attached to the performance of the daily task, the next step was for the autonomous individual to regard his achievements as a quasi-divine mastering of the environment. It is likely that this secularisation of the Calvinist conception of stewardship was of considerable importance for the rise of the novel. *Robinson Crusoe* is certainly the first novel in the sense that it is the first fictional narrative in which an ordinary person's daily activities are the centre of continuous literary attention. These activities, it is true, are not seen in a wholly secular light; but later novelists could continue Defoe's serious concern with man's worldly doings without placing them in a religious framework. It is therefore likely that the Puritan conception of the dignity of labour helped to bring into being the novel's general premise that the individual's daily life is of sufficient importance and interest to be the proper subject of literature.

III

Economic individualism explains much of Crusoe's character; economic specialisation and its associated ideology help to account for the appeal of his adventures; but it is Puritan individualism which controls his spiritual being.

Troeltsch has claimed that "the really permanent attainment of individualism was due to a religious, and not a secular movement, to the Reformation and not the Renaissance." It is neither feasible nor profitable to attempt to establish priorities in such matters, but it is certainly true that if there is one element which all forms of Protestantism have in common it is the replacement of the rule of the Church as the mediator between man and God by another view of religion in which it is the individual who is entrusted with the primary responsibility for his own spiritual direction. Two aspects of this new Protestant emphasis—the tendency to increase consciousness of the self as a spiritual entity, and the tendency to a kind of democratisation of the moral and social outlook—are particularly important both to *Robinson Crusoe* and to the development of the presuppositions on which the formal realism of the novel is based.

The idea of religous self-scrutiny as an important duty for each individual is, of course, much older than Protestantism; it derives from the individualist and subjective emphasis of primitive Christianity, and finds its supreme expression in St. Augustine's *Confessions*. But it is generally agreed that it was Calvin, in the sixteenth century, who re-established and systematised this earlier pattern of purposive spiritual introspection, and made it the supreme religious ritual for the layman as well as for the priest: every good Puritan conducted a continual scrutiny of his inner man for evidence of his own place in the divine plot of election and reprobation.

This "internalisation of conscience" is everywhere manifested in Calvinism. In New England, it has been said, "almost every literate Puritan kept some sort of journal"; and, in England, *Grace Abounding* is the great monument of a way of life which Bunyan shared with the other members of his sect, the Baptists, who were, with one or two minor additions and subtractions, orthodox Calvinists. In later generations the introspective habit remained even where religious conviction weakened, and there resulted the three greatest autobiographical confessions of the modern period, those of Pepys, Rousseau and Boswell, all of whom were brought up under the Calvinist discipline; their fascination with self-analysis, and indeed their extreme egocentricity, are character traits which they shared both with later Calvinism in general and with Defoe's heroes.

(a)

The importance of this subjective and individualist spiritual pattern to Defoe's work, and to the rise of the novel, is very evident. *Robinson Crusoe* initiates that aspect of the novel's treatment of experience which rivals the confessional autobiography and outdoes other literary forms in bringing us close to the inward moral being of the individual; and it achieves this closeness to the inner life of the protagonist by using as formal basis the autobiographical memoir which was the most immediate and widespread literary expression of the introspective tendency of Puritanism in general.

Defoe himself, of course, was born and bred a Puritan. His father was a Dissenter, perhaps a Baptist, more probably a Presbyterian, in any case a Calvinist; and he sent his son to a dissenting academy, probably intending him for the ministry. Defoe's own religious beliefs changed a good deal, and he expressed in his writings the whole gamut of doctrines, from intransigent predestinarianism to rational deism, which Puritanism held during its varied course of development; nevertheless, there is no doubt that Defoe remained and was generally considered to be a Dissenter, and that much of the outlook revealed in his novels is distinctively Puritan.

There is nothing to suggest that Robinson Crusoe was intended to be a Dissenter. On the other hand, the note of his religious reflections is often Puritan in character—their tenor has been seen by one theologian as very close to the Presbyterian Shorter Catechism of the 1648 Westminster Assembly. Crusoe certainly exhibits frequent signs of bibliolatry: he quotes some twenty verses of the Bible in the first part of *Robinson Crusoe* alone, besides making many briefer references; and he sometimes seeks divine guidance by opening the Bible at random. But the most significant aspect of his spiritual life is his tendency to rigorous moral and religious self-examination. Each of his actions is followed by a passage of reflection in which Crusoe ponders over the problem of how it reveals the intentions of divine providence. If the corn sprouts, it is surely a divine miracle "so directed for my sustenance"; if he has a bout of fever "a leisurely review of the miseries of death" eventually convinces him that he deserves reprobation for neglecting to show his gratitude for God's mercies to him. The modern reader no doubt tends to pay little attention to these parts of the narrative; but Crusoe and his author showed their point of view very clearly by allotting the spiritual realm as much importance as the practical, both in space and emphasis. It would therefore appear that what are probably the vestigial remnants of the Calvinist introspective discipline helped to provide us for the first time in the history of fiction with a hero whose day-by-day mental and moral life is fully shared by the reader.

This crucial literary advance was not, of course, brought about by the introspective tendency of Puritanism alone. As we have seen, the gospel of work had a similar effect in giving the individual's daily economic task almost as much importance as his daily spiritual self-examination; and the parallel effects of both these tendencies were supplemented by another closely related tendency in Puritanism.

If God had given the individual prime responsibility for his own spiritual destiny, it followed that he must have made this possible by signifying his intentions to the individual in the events of his daily life. The Puritan therefore tended to see every item in his personal experience as potentially rich in moral and spiritual meaning; and Defoe's hero is acting according to this tradition when he tries to interpret so many of the mundane events of the narrative as divine pointers which may help him to find his own place in the eternal scheme of redemption and reprobation.

In that scheme, of course, all souls had equal chances, and it therefore followed that the individual had as full an opportunity of showing his spiritual qualities in the ordinary conduct of life as in its rarer and more dramatic exigencies. This was one reason for the general Puritan tendency towards the democratisation of the moral and social scale, and it was assisted by several other factors. There were, for instance, many social, moral and political reasons why the Puritans should be hostile to the aristocratic scale of values; nor could they fail to disapprove of its literary expression in the traditional heroes of romance, extrovert conquerors whose victories are won, not in the spirit or in the counting-house but on the battlefield and in the boudoir. It is at all events clear that Puritanism brought about a fundamental and in a sense democratic orientation in the social and literary outlook of its adherents, an orientation which was described by Milton's lines in *Paradise Lost:* "To know / That which before us lies in daily life / Is the prime wisdom," and which evoked one of Defoe's most eloquent pieces of writing, an essay in *Applebee's Journal* (1722) on the funeral of Marlborough. The essay's peroration begins:

> What then is the work of life? What the business of great men, that pass the stage of the world in seeming triumph as these men, we call heroes, have done? Is it to grow great in the mouth of fame, and take up many pages in history? Alas! that is no more than makng a tale for the reading of posterity, till it turns into fable and romance. Is it to furnish subject to the poets, and live in their immortal rhymes, as they call them? That is, in short, no more than to be hereafter turned into ballad and song, and be sung by old women to quiet children; or, at the corner of a street, to gather crowds in aid of the pickpocket and the whore. Or is their business rather to add virtue and piety to their glory, which alone will pass them into Eternity, and make them truly immortal? What is glory without virtue? A great man without religion is no more than a great beast without a soul.

Then Defoe modulates into something more like the narrowly ethical evaluation of merit which was to be one of the legacies of Puritanism to the middle-class code: "What is honour without merit? And what can be called true merit, but that which makes a person a good man, as well as a great man."

Neither Crusoe, nor indeed any of Defoe's heroes, it must be admitted, are conspicuous by these standards of virtue, religion, merit and goodness; and, of course, Defoe did not intend them to be so. But these standards do represent the moral plane on which Defoe's novels exist, and by which his heroes must be judged: the ethical scale has been so internalised and democratised, that unlike the scale of achievement common in epic or romance, it is relevant to the lives and actions of ordinary people. In this Defoe's heroes are typical of the later characters of the novel: Robinson Crusoe, Moll Flanders and even Colonel Jacque never think of glory or honour; they have their being on the moral plane of day-to-day living more completely than those of previous narratives, and their thoughts and actions only exhibit an ordinary, a democratic goodness and badness. Robinson Crusoe, for instance, is Defoe's most heroic character, but there is nothing unusual about his personality or the way he faces his strange experiences; as Coleridge pointed out, he is essentially "the universal representative, the person, for whom every reader could substitute himself . . . nothing is done, thought, suffered, or desired, but what every man can imagine himself doing, thinking, feeling, or wishing for."

Defoe's presentation of Robinson Crusoe as the "universal representative" is intimately connected with the egalitarian tendency of Puritanism in yet another way. For not only did this tendency make the way the individual faced every problem of everyday life a matter of deep and continuing spiritual concern; it also encouraged a literary outlook which was suited to describing such problems with the most detailed fidelity.

In *Mimesis,* a brilliant panorama of realistic representation in literature from Homer to Virginia Woolf, Erich Auerbach has demonstrated the general connection between the Christian view of man and the serious literary portrayal of ordinary people and of common life. The classical theory of genres had reflected the social and philosophical orientation of Greece and Rome: tragedy described the heroic vicissitudes of people better than ourselves in appropriately elevated language, whereas the domain of everyday reality belonged to comedy which was supposed to portray people "inferior to ourselves" in an appropriately "low" style. Christian literature, however, reflecting a very different social and philosophical outlook, had no place for this *Stiltrennung* or segregation of styles according to the class status of the subject-matter. The gospel narratives treated the doings of humble people with the utmost seriousness and on occasion, indeed, with sublimity; later, this tradition was continued in many of the mediaeval literary forms, from the lives of the saints to the miracle plays; and it eventually found its greatest expression in Dante's *Divina Commedia*.

The classicising tendencies of the Renaissance and the Counter-Reformation, however, re-established the old doctrine of genre, and indeed elaborated it to an extent that would certainly have surprised Aristotle. The supreme example of this elaboration is found in French literature of the seventeenth century, and especially in tragedy; not only was the unremitting use of a fully codified style noble pre-scribed, but even the objects and actions of everyday life were banished from the stage.

In Protestant countries, however, the *Stiltrennung* never achieved such authority, especially in England where neoclassicism was con-fronted by the example of Shakespeare and that characteristic min-gling of the tragic and comic modes which was part of his legacy from the Middle Ages. Nevertheless, in one important respect even Shakespeare followed the *Stiltrennung:* his treatment of low and rus-tic characters is very similar to that of the protagonists of the neo-classical tradition from Ben Jonson to Dryden, and there is nothing egalitarian about it. It is very significant that the main exceptions to this derogatory attitude are found in the works of Puritan writers. In Adam, Milton created the first epic hero who is essentially a "uni-versal representative"; Bunyan, seeing all souls as equal before God, accorded the humble and their lives a much more serious and sym-pathetic attention than they received in the other literature of his period; while the works of Defoe are the supreme illustration in the novel of the connection between the democratic individualism of Puritanism and the objective representation of the world of everyday reality and all those who inhabit it.

(b)

There is a great difference, however, between Bunyan and Defoe, a difference which suggests why it is Defoe, rather than Bunyan, who is often considered to be our first novelist. In the earlier fiction of the Puritan movement—in such works as Arthur Dent's *Plain Man's Pathway to Heaven,* or the stories of Bunyan and his Baptist confrère Benjamin Keach—we have many elements of the novel: simple language, realistic descriptions of persons and places, and a serious presentation of the moral problems of ordinary individuals. But the significance of the characters and their actions largely depends upon a transcendental scheme of things: to say that the persons are allegorical is to say that their earthly reality is not the main object of the writer, but rather that he hopes to make us see through them a larger and unseen reality beyond time and place.

In Defoe's novels, on the other hand, although religious concerns are present they have no such priority of status: indeed the heritage of Puritanism is demonstrably too weak to supply a continuous and controlling pattern for the hero's experience. If, for example, we turn to the actual effect of Crusoe's religion on his behaviour, we find that it has curiously little. Defoe often suggests that an incident is an act of Divine providence or retribution, but this interpretation is rarely supported by the facts of the story. To take the crucial instance: if Crusoe's original sin was filial disobedience—leaving home in the first place—it is certain that no real retribution follows, since he does very well out of it; and later he often sets out for further journeys without any fear that he may be flouting Providence. This indeed comes very near to the "neglect" of the "Cautions, warning and instruction . . . Providence" which Crusoe called a "kind of Practical Atheism" in his *Serious Reflections*. Where Providence is bringing blessings—as, for instance, when he finds the grains of corn and rice—things are different: Crusoe need only accept. But the trilogy as a whole certainly suggests that any of the less cooperative interventions of Providence can safely be neglected.

Marx sourly noted this somewhat gratuitous character of Crusoe's religious life. "Of his prayers we take no account, since they are a source of pleasure to him, and he looks on them as so much recreation." He would have been pleased to find that Gildon thought that the "religious and useful reflections" were "in reality . . . put in . . . to swell the bulk of Defoe's treatise to a five-shilling book." Both Marx and Gildon were right in drawing attention to the discontinuity between the religious aspects of the book and its action: but their explanations do Defoe some injustice. His spiritual intentions were probably quite sincere, but they have the weakness of all "Sunday religion" and manifest themselves in somewhat unconvincing periodical tributes to the transcendent at times when a respite from real action and practical intellectual effort is allowed or enforced. Such, certainly, is Crusoe's religion, and we feel that it is in the last analysis the result of an unresolved and probably unconscious conflict in Defoe himself. He lived fully in the sphere of practical and utilitarian action, and could be wholly true to his being when he described this aspect of Robinson Crusoe's life. But his religious upbringing forced him from time to time to hand over a brilliant piece of narrative by a star-reporter to a distant colleague on the religious page who could be relied on to supply suitable spiritual commentaries quickly out of stock. Puritanism made the editorial policy unalterable; but it was usually satisfied by a purely formal adherence. In this, too, Defoe is typical of the development of Puritanism; in the phrase of H. W. Schneider, "beliefs seldom become doubts; they become ritual." Otherworldly concerns do not provide the essential themes of Defoe's novels: but they do punctuate the narrative with comminatory codas that demonstrate a lifetime of somewhat mechanical practice.

The relative impotence of religion in Defoe's novels, then, suggests not insincerity but the profound secularisation of his outlook, a secularisation which was a marked feature of his age—the word itself in its modern sense dates from the first decades of the eighteenth century. Defoe himself had been born at a time when the Puritan Commonwealth had just collapsed at the Restoration, while *Robinson Crusoe* was written in the year of the Salters' Hall controversy, when, after the last hopes of Dissent in a compromise with the Anglican Church had been given up, even their effort to unite among themselves proved impossible. In the *Serious Reflections of Robinson Crusoe* Defoe's hero meditates on the ebbing of the Christian religion throughout the world; it is a bitterly divided minority force in a largely pagan world, and God's final intervention seems remoter than ever. Such, at least, is the conclusion to which Robinson Crusoe is forced by his own experience in the last words of the book:

> No such zeal for the Christian religion will be found in our days, or perhaps in any age of the world, till Heaven beats the drums itself, and the glorious legions from above come down on purpose to propagate the work, and reduce the whole world to the obedience of King Jesus—a time which some tell us is not far off, but of which I heard nothing in all my travels and illuminations, no, not one word.

"No, not one word": the dying fall leaves Crusoe to his despair. What he was told to expect and what he has experienced do not agree. Until heaven beats the drums itself he must reconcile himself to a pilgrim's progress through an effectively secular world, make his own way along a path no longer clearly illumined by God's particular providences.

The causes of secularisation in the period are many, but one of the most important, especially as far as Puritanism is concerned, was economic and social progress. In New England, for instance, the Pilgrim Fathers soon forgot that they had originally founded "a plantation of religion, not a plantation of Trades"; and it has been said that Governor Bradford, in his *History of Plymouth Plantation,* shows how a Puritan saint came to write "less and less like a Puritan preacher and more and more like the author of *Robinson Crusoe."* In England, by Defoe's time, the more respectable dissenting sects at least were dominated by wealthy and somewhat time-serving merchants and financiers; and opportunities for further gain drove many prosperous Dissenters not only to occasional conformity, but into the Anglican Church. In his early years Defoe had violently denounced occasional conformity, but Robinson Crusoe, we notice, is an occasional conformist with a vengeance—he even passes as a Papist when it is economically expedient to do so.

The conflict between spiritual and material values is an old one, but it was perhaps more obvious in the eighteenth century than at any other time; more obvious because so many people thought, apparently in perfectly good faith, that it did not really exist. Bishop Warburton, for example, argued that "to provide for utility is, at the same time, to provide for truth, its inseparable associate." The reluctance to consider the extent to which spiritual and material values may be opposed is very marked in Defoe's novels, and it can even be argued that the crucial critical problem which they raise is whether they do not in fact confuse the whole issue. But, whatever our decision on this point, it is at least clear that the mere possibility of such a confusion only exists because Defoe presents us with a narrative in which both "high" and "low" motives are treated with equal seriousness: the moral continuum of his novels is much closer than was that of any previous fiction to the complex combination of spiritual and material issues which moral choices in daily life customarily involve.

It would seem, then, that Defoe's importance in the history of the novel is directly connected with the way his narrative structure embodied the struggle between Puritanism and the tendency to secularisation which was rooted in material progress. At the same time it is also apparent that the secular and economic viewpoint is the dominant partner, and that it is this which explains why it is Defoe, rather than Bunyan, who is usually considered to be the first key figure in the rise of the novel.

De Vogüé, the Catholic opponent of the French Realists, found an atheistic presumption in the novel's exclusion of the non-natural; and it is certain that the novel's usual means—formal realism—tends to exclude whatever is not vouched for by the senses: the jury does not normally allow divine intervention as an explanation of human actions. It is therefore likely that a measure of seclarisation was an indispensable condition for the rise of the new genre. The novel could only concentrate on personal relations once most writers and readers believed that individual human beings, and not collectivities such as the Church, or transcendent actors, such as the Persons of the Trinity, were allotted the supreme role on the earthly stage. The novel, Georg Lukács has written, is the epic of a world forsaken by God; it presents, in de Sade's phrase, "le tableau des mœurs séculaires."

This, of course, is not to say that the novelist himself or his novel cannot be religious, but only that whatever the ends of the novelist may be, his means should be rigidly restricted to terrestrial characters and actions: the realm of the spirit should be presented only through the subjective experiences of the characters. Thus Dostoevsky's novels, for example, in no sense depend for their verisimilitude or their significance on his religious views; divine intervention is not a necessary construct for an adequate and complete explanation of the causes and meanings of each action, as it is in Bunyan. Alyosha and Father Zossima are portrayed very objectively: indeed, the very brilliance of Dostoevsky's presentation shows that he cannot assume, but must prove, the reality of the spirit: and *The Brothers Karamazov* as a whole does not depend upon any non-naturalistic causation or significance to be effective and complete.

To sum up, we can say that the novel requires a world view which is centred on the social relationships between individual persons; and this involves secularisation as well as individualism, because until the end of the seventeenth century the individual was not conceived as wholly autonomous, but as an element in a picture which depended on divine persons for its meaning, as well as on traditional institutions such as Church and Kingship for its secular pattern.

At the same time the positive contribution of Puritanism, not only to the development of modern individualism but to the rise of the novel, and to its later tradition in England, must not be under-estimated. It was through Puritanism that Defoe brought into the novel a treatment of the individual's psychological concerns that was a tremendous advance in the kind of forensic ratiocination which had previously passed for psychological description in even the best of the romances, such as those of Madame de La Fayette. Nor does the fact that, in the words of Rudolph Stamm, who has given the most complete account of Defoe's religious position, Defoe's writings show that his "own experience of reality had nothing in common with that of a believing Calvinist" disprove the positive importance of Defoe's dissenting background. For we can say of him, as of later novelists in the same tradition, such as Samuel Richardson, George Eliot or D. H. Lawrence, that they have inherited of Puritanism everything except its religious faith. They all have an intensely active conception of life as a continuous moral and social struggle; they all see every event in ordinary life as proposing an intrinsically moral issue on which reason and conscience must be exerted to the full before right action is possible; they all seek by introspection and observation to build their own personal scheme of moral certainty; and in different ways they all manifest the self-righteous and some-what angular individualism of the earlier Puritan character.

IV

We have until now been primarily concerned with the light which Defoe's first work of fiction sheds on the nature of the con-nections between economic and religious individualism and the rise of the novel; but since the primary reason for our interest in *Robinson Crusoe* is its literary greatness, the relation between that greatness and the way it reflects the deepest aspirations and dilemmas of individ-ualism also requires brief consideration.

Robinson Crusoe falls most naturally into place, not with other novels, but with the great myths of Western civilisation, with *Faust, Don Juan* and *Don Quixote*. All these have as their basic plots, their enduring images, a single-minded pursuit by the protagonist of one of the characteristic desires of Western man. Each of their heroes embodies an *arete* and a *hubris,* an exceptional prowess and a vitiating excess, in spheres of action that are particularly important in our culture. Don Quixote, the impetuous generosity and the limiting blindness of chivalric idealism; Don Juan, pursuing and at the same time tormented by the idea of boundless experience of women; Faustus, the great knower, his curiosity always unsatisfied, and therefore damned. Crusoe, of course, seems to insist that he is not of their company; *they* are very exceptional people, whereas anyone would do what *he* did, in the circumstances. Yet he too has an exceptional prowess; he can manage quite on his own. And he has an excess: his inordinate egocentricity condemns him to isolation wherever he is.

The egocentricity, one might say, is forced on him, because he is cast away on an island. But it is also true that his character is throughout courting its fate and it merely happens that the island offers the fullest opportunity for him to realise three associated tendencies of modern civilisation—absolute economic, social and intellectual freedom for the individual.

It was Crusoe's realisation of intellectual freedom which made Rousseau propose the book as "the one book that teaches all that books can teach" for the education of Emile; he argued that "the surest way to raise oneself above prejudices, and order one's judgement on the real relationship between things, is to put oneself in the place of an isolated man, and to judge of everything as that man would judge of them according to their actual usefulness."

On his island Crusoe also enjoys the absolute freedom from social restrictions for which Rousseau yearned—there are no family ties or civil authorities to interfere with his individual autonomy. Even when he is no longer alone his personal autarchy remains—indeed it is increased: the parrot cries out his master's name; unprompted Friday swears to be his slave for ever; Crusoe toys with the fancy that he is an absolute monarch; and one of his visitors even wonders if he is a god.

Lastly, Crusoe's island gives him the complete laissez-faire which economic man needs to realise his aims. At home market conditions, taxation and problems of the labour supply make it impossible for the individual to control every aspect of production, distribution and exchange. The conclusion is obvious. Follow the call of the wide open places, discover an island that is desert only because it is barren of owners or competitors, and there build your personal Empire with the help of a Man Friday who needs no wages and makes it much easier to support the white man's burden.

Such is the positive and prophetic side of Defoe's story, the side which makes Crusoe an inspiration to economists and educators, and a symbol both for the displaced persons of urban capitalism, such as Rousseau, and for its more practical heroes, the empire builders. Crusoe realises all these ideal freedoms, and in doing so he is undoubtedly a distinctively modern culture-hero. Aristotle, for example, who thought that the man "who is unable to live in society, or who has no need because he is sufficient for himself, must be either a beast or a god," would surely have found Crusoe a very strange hero. Perhaps with reason; for it is surely true that the ideal freedoms he achieves are both quite impracticable in the real world and in so far as they can be applied, disastrous for human happiness.

It may be objected that Robinson Crusoe's achievements are credible and wholly convincing. This is so, but only because in his narrative—perhaps as an unconscious victim of what Karl Mannheim has called the "Utopian mentality" which is dominated by its will to action and consequently "turns its back on everything which would shake its belief"—Defoe disregarded two important facts: the social nature of all human economies, and the actual psychological effects of solitude.

The basis for Robinson Crusoe's prosperity, of course, is the original stock of tools which he loots from the shipwreck; they comprise, we are told, "the biggest magazine of all kinds . . . that was ever laid up for one man." So Defoe's hero is not really a primitive nor a proletarian but a capitalist. In the island he owns the freehold of a rich though unimproved estate. Its possession, combined with the stock from the ship, are the miracles which fortify the faith of the supporters of the new economic creed. But only that of the true believers: to the sceptic the classic idyll of free enterprise does not in fact sustain the view that anyone has ever attained comfort and security only by his own efforts. Crusoe is in fact the lucky heir to the labours of countless other individuals; his solitude is the measure, and the price of his luck, since it involves the fortunate decease of all the other potential stockholders; and the shipwreck, far from being a tragic peripety, is the deus ex machina which makes it possible for Defoe to present solitary labour, not as an alternative to a death sentence, but as a solution to the perplexities of economic and social reality.

The psychological objection to *Robinson Crusoe* as a pattern of action is also obvious. Just as society has made every individual what he is, so the prolonged lack of society actually tends to make the individual relapse into a straightened primitivism of thought and feeling. In Defoe's sources for *Robinson Crusoe* what actually happened to the castaways was at best uninspiring. At worst, harassed by fear and dogged by ecological degradation, they sank more and more to the level of animals, lost the use of speech, went mad, or died of inanition. One book which Defoe had almost certainly read, *The Voyages and Travels of J. Albert de Mandelslo,* tells of two such cases; of a Frenchman who, after only two years of solitude on Mauritius, tore his clothing to pieces in a fit of madness brought on by a diet of raw tortoise; and of a Dutch seaman on St. Helena who disinterred the body of a buried comrade and set out to sea in the coffin.

These realities of absolute solitude were in keeping with the traditional view of its effects, as expressed by Dr. Johnson: the "solitary mortal," he averred, was "certainly luxurious, probably superstitious, and possibly mad: the mind stagnates for want of employment; grows morbid, and is extinguished like a candle in foul air."

In the story just the opposite happens: Crusoe turns his forsaken estate into a triumph. Defoe departs from psychological probability in order to redeem his picture of man's inexorable solitariness, and it is for this reason that he appeals very strongly to all who feel isolated—and who at times does not? An inner voice continually suggests to us that the human isolation which individualism has fostered is painful and tends ultimately to a life of apathetic animality and mental derangement; Defoe answers confidently that it can be made the arduous prelude to the fuller realisation of every individual's potentialities; and the solitary readers of two centuries of individualism cannot but applaud so convincing an example of making a virtue out of a necessity, so cheering a colouring to that universal image of individualist experience, solitude.

That it is universal—the word that is always to be found inscribed on the other side of the coin of individualism—can hardly be doubted. We have already seen how, although Defoe himself was an optimistic spokesman of the new economic and social order, the unreflecting veracity of his vision as a novelist led him to report many of the less inspiring phenomena associated with economic individualism which tended to isolate man from his family and his country. Modern sociologists have attributed very similar consequences to the other two major trends which are reflected in *Robinson*

Crusoe. Max Weber, for example, has shown how the religious individualism of Calvin created among its adherents a historically unprecedented "inner isolation"; while Emile Durkheim derived from the division of labour and its associated changes many of the endless conflicts and complexities of the norms of modern society, the anomie which sets the individual on his own and, incidentally, provides the novelists with a rich mine of individual and social problems when he portrays the life of his time.

Defoe himself seems to have been much more aware of the larger representativeness of his epic of solitude than is commonly assumed. Not wholly aware, since, as we have seen, he departed from its actual economic and psychological effects to make his hero's struggles more cheering than they might otherwise have been; nevertheless Crusoe's most eloquent utterances are concerned with solitude as the universal state of man.

The *Serious Reflections of Robinson Crusoe* (1720) are actually a miscellaneous compilation of religious, moral and thaumaturgic material, and cannot, as a whole, be taken seriously as a part of the story: the volume was primarily put together to cash in on the great success of the first part of the trilogy, *The Life and Strange Surprising Adventures,* and the smaller one of the *Further Adventures.* There are, however, in the prefaces, and the first essay, "On Solitude," a number of valuable clues as to what, on second thoughts at least, Defoe saw as the meaning of his hero's experiences.

In "Robinson Crusoe's Preface" he suggests that the story "though allegorical, is also historical": it is based on the life of "a man alive, and well known too, the actions of whose life are the just subject of these volumes, and to whom all or most part of the story most directly alludes"; and Defoe hints that he is himself the "original" of which Robinson Crusoe is the "emblem"; that it is his own life which he is portraying allegorically.

Many critics have denied, and even derided the claim. *Robinson Crusoe* had apparently been attacked as fictitious, and it is argued that Defoe was merely using the allegorical argument very largely to controvert this criticism, and also to alleviate the popular Puritan aversion to fiction which he largely shared. Still, the claim to some autobiographical relevance cannot be wholly rejected: *Robinson Crusoe* is the only book for which he made the claim; and it fits in very well with much of what we know of Defoe's outlook and aspirations.

Defoe was himself an isolated and solitary figure in his time;

witness the summary of his own life which he wrote in the preface
to a 1706 pamphlet, *A Reply to a Pamphlet, Entitled "The Lord
Haversham's Vindication of His Speech . . ."* where he complains

> how I stand alone in the world, abandoned by those very
> people that own I have done them service; . . . how, with
> . . . no helps but my own industry, I have forced misfor-
> tune, and reduced them, exclusive of composition, from
> seventeen to less than five thousand pounds; how, in gaols,
> in retreats, in all manner of extremities, I have supported
> myself without the assistance of friends or relations.

"Forcing his way with undiscouraged diligence" is surely the hero-
ism which Crusoe shares with his creator: and in "Robinson Crusoe's
Preface" it is this quality which he mentions as the inspiring theme
of his book: "Here is invincible patience recommended under the
worst of misery, indefatigable application and undaunted resolution
under the greatest and most discouraging circumstances."

Having asserted an autobiographical meaning for his story,
Defoe goes on to consider the problem of solitude. His discussion is
an interesting illustration of Weber's view of the effects of Calvinism. Most of the argument is concerned with the Puritan insistence
on the need for the individual to overcome the world in his own
soul, to achieve a spiritual solitude without recourse to monasticism.
"The business is to get a retired soul," he says, and goes on: "All the
parts of a complete solitude are to be as effectually enjoyed, if we
please, and sufficient grace assisting, even in the most populous cities, among the hurries of conversation and gallantry of a court, or the
noise and business of a camp, as in the deserts of Arabia and Lybia,
or in the desolate life of an uninhabited island."

This note, however, occasionally relapses into a more general
statement of solitude as an enduring psychological fact: "All reflection is carried home, and our dear self is, in one respect, the end of
living. Hence man may be properly said to be alone in the midst of
crowds and the hurry of men and business. All the reflections which
he makes are to himself; all that is pleasant he embraces for himself;
all that is irksome and grievous is tasted but by his own palate." Here
the Puritan insistence on possessing one's soul intact from a sinful
world is couched in terms which suggest a more absolute, secular
and personal alienation from society. Later this echo of the redefined
aloneness of Descartes's *solus ipse* modulates into an anguished sense

of personal loneliness whose overpowering reality moves Defoe to
his most urgent and moving eloquence:

> What are the sorrows of other men to us, and what their
> joy? Something we may be touched indeed with by the
> power of sympathy, and a secret turn of the affections; but
> all the solid reflection is directed to ourselves. Our medi-
> tations are all solitude in perfection; our passions are all
> exercised in retirement; we love, we hate, we covet, we
> enjoy, all in privacy and solitude. All that we communi-
> cate of those things to any other is but for their assistance
> in the pursuit of our desires; the end is at home; the en-
> joyment, the contemplation, is all solitude and retirement;
> it is for ourselves we enjoy, and for ourselves we suffer.

"We covet, we enjoy, all in privacy and solitude": what really occupies man is something that makes him solitary wherever he is, and
too aware of the interested nature of any relationship with other
human beings to find any consolation there. "All that we commu-
nicate . . . to any other is but for their assistance in the pursuit of our
desires": a rationally conceived self-interest makes a mockery of
speech; and the scene of Crusoe's silent life is not least a Utopia
because its functional silence, broken only by an occasional "Poor
Robinson Crusoe" from the parrot, does not impose upon man's
ontological egocentricity the need to assume a false façade of social
intercourse, or to indulge in the mockery of communication with his
fellows.

Robinson Crusoe, then, presents a monitory image of the ultimate
consequences of absolute individualism. But this tendency, like all
extreme tendencies, soon provoked a reaction. As soon as man's
aloneness was forced on the attention of mankind, the close and
complex nature of the individual's dependence on society, which had
been taken for granted until it was challenged by individualism,
began to receive much more detailed analysis. Man's essentially social nature, for instance, became one of the main topics of the
eighteenth-century philosophers; and the greatest of them, David
Hume, wrote in the *Treatise of Human Nature* (1739) a passage which
might almost have been a refutation of *Robinson Crusoe:*

> We can form no wish which has not a reference to soci-
> ety. . . . Let all the powers and elements of nature conspire

to serve and obey one man; let the sun rise and set at his command; the sea and rivers roll as he pleases, and the earth still furnish spontaneously whatever may be useful or agreeable to him; he will still be miserable, till you give him one person at least with whom he may share his happiness, and whose esteem and friendship he may enjoy.

Just as the modern study of society only began once individualism had focussed attention on man's apparent disjunctions from his fellows, so the novel could only begin its study of personal relationships once *Robinson Crusoe* had revealed a solitude that cried aloud for them. Defoe's story is perhaps not a novel in the usual sense since it deals so little with personal relations. But it is appropriate that the tradition of the novel should begin with a work that annihilated the relationships of the traditional social order, and thus drew attention to the opportunity and the need of building up a network of personal relationships on a new and conscious pattern; the terms of the problem of the novel and of modern thought alike were established when the old order of moral and social relationships was shipwrecked, with Robinson Crusoe, by the rising tide of individualism.

Crusoe and Spiritual Autobiography

G. A. Starr

Discussions of *Robinson Crusoe* commonly focus on the island existence, and the "original sin" has also attracted attention, but the
intervening wanderings tend to be passed over. Considered simply
as narrative, however, this phase of the book deserves some scrutiny,
for from one point of view it is curiously brief, from another it is
oddly extended. Why does Defoe have so little to say about Sallee
and Brazil, and yet detain Crusoe so long from reaching the island?
For all his interest in circumstantial realism, Defoe takes few pains to
"place" Crusoe in Sallee, about which there was a considerable literature, or in Brazil, which was also adequately described. Crusoe's
stay in Sallee occupies less than five pages, which mainly concern his
devices to escape; little is said about the city or his life there, and even
less space is devoted to his four years in Brazil. In such travel-
narratives as *Captain Singleton* and the *Farther Adventures of Robinson
Crusoe,* Defoe's zest for factual detail seldom flags; in this book, it is
largely reserved for the island. Despite the availability of ample material on Barbary slavery and Brazilian settlements, he neglects these
opportunities to display his powers of narrative realism.

It could be argued that he is primarily concerned to get Crusoe
to the island, but that, to bring him into the neighborhood with
some show of plausibility, he must contrive this sequence of preliminary stages. Robert Drury can be shipwrecked on Madagascar within
thirteen pages of the beginning of a book because Madagascar is in
fact on the route to India; if Crusoe is to be isolated from the normal

From *Defoe and Spiritual Autobiography.* © 1965 by Princeton University Press.

paths of commerce the preparations have to be rather more elaborate.

But there are other reasons, I think, why it is nearly fifty pages
before Crusoe clambers ashore on his island. For one thing, his
habitat becomes more and more remote from his native Yorkshire,
until at last it is a place found on no map. Earlier discussion of the
Account showed how the author, who in fact remains in London
throughout the book, expresses his estrangement from God through
metaphors of physical distance: he speaks of himself as wandering,
straying, fleeing, hiding, and rambling in order to convey his inward, spiritual remoteness from "the true center of his being." What
we have in Crusoe's case, I think, is a full enactment of this process
in the outward narrative. Instead of merely likening himself to one in
this predicament, Crusoe actually undergoes such wanderings, yet
they seem to retain their traditional overtones of alienation. The
background of this identification between literal and spiritual wandering has already been presented and need not be recapitulated;
instead we may turn to another possible reason for Crusoe's delay in
reaching the island.

However impious and imprudent it may be, his decision to
venture abroad is entirely voluntary; he is neither tricked like Colonel Jack nor forced by law like Moll Flanders into embarking on his
voyage. Nevertheless he has remarkably little control over the direction of his travels. Not only is his judgment tainted, even at the
time of his initial misstep, but choice of any kind, rational or otherwise, has less and less power over his affairs. This process of sub-
jection, first of reason to rebellious inclination, next of action in
general to external circumstances, traditionally marks the worsening
predicament of unregenerate man.

That Crusoe actually undergoes such a process can perhaps be
best illustrated by the Barbary slavery episode. In attempting to
repeat the success of his first trading voyage to Guinea, he is captured
by pirates and carried to Sallee. As already indicated, Defoe shows
little interest in developing the narrative possibilities of Crusoe's
captivity, although model accounts were available to him, and he
had long been interested in African affairs. There was one feature of
the slavery accounts, however, which was more to Defoe's purpose
than their descriptive details. They all tended to be written from the
same motives: namely, to return thanks for the author's ultimate
escape or redemption, and to celebrate the workings of a beneficent

Providence even amid the remote, benighted Moors. Even when the bulk of a narrative consisted of exotic topography, fabulous natural history, and prodigious action, as in *The Adventures of Mr. T. S. an English Merchant* (1670), it was deemed appropriate to begin as follows: "There is nothing appears more wonderful than Gods Providence in the Governance of the World, and in the disposition of Mankind; it carries us through various Estates; it brings us in Dangers and Miseries, and in a due time leads us out again by means not discoverable to our shallow foresight; it causeth us to meet with such different Accidents, which some may attribute to Chance; but if we take the pains to examine and question them, we shall find them to be appointed by a Divine Wisdom for the Publick and our own Advantage. . . . Modern and Ancient Histories are full of such strange Examples of the Proceedings of Providence, which tend many times only to fashion and frame us to a certain temper that may make us more useful in our Generations."

Now this is just the kind of reflection that Crusoe comes to make after his conversion, but at the time of his captivity and escape he is blind to the agency of Providence in his affairs. He does feel at first that "now the hand of heaven had overtaken me, and I was undone without redemption," but beyond this he makes no spiritual "improvement" of his situation. When he does manage to escape, a north-north-east wind blows him down the African coast, away from Sallee but also away from Europe: "my resolutions were," he says, "blow which way it would, I would be gone from the horrid place where I was, and leave the rest to Fate." His own power of choice, which had misled him initially when exercised in disregard of, and in conflict with, his providentially ordered role, is thus overruled and supplanted by the force of circumstances. Nor has he the merit in this instance of deferring to the superior will of Providence; on the contrary, he recognizes no higher power at work than "Fate." As he later reflects on his ensuing adventures: "When I was on the desperate expedition on the desert shores of Africa, I never had so much as one thought of what would become of me; or one wish to God to direct me whither I should go, or to keep me from the danger which apparently surrounded me, as well from voracious creatures as cruel savages. But I was merely thoughtless of a God or a Providence; acted like a mere brute from the principles of Nature, and by the dictates of common sense only, and indeed hardly that." Having cast off the submission he owes to paternal and divine authority, he finds no real freedom in its place. Not only in the period of literal slavery, but throughout these wanderings, he is mastered by events rather than master of them.

What might appear to be exceptions to this pattern tend only to confirm it. Crusoe may be said to exercise choice when he reembarks from London after the first shipwreck in Yarmouth Roads; when he sets up as a Brazilian planter rather than returning to England; and when he decides to undertake the slaving voyage. But each of these decisions only deepens the guilt of his original mischoice. They do this first by repeating and confirming the substance of the original sin—that is, by obeying unruly inclination rather than reason and duty, and thus drawing what might have seemed a momentary lapse into a settled habit of conduct; and, second, by adding further dimensions to the original sin, for to headstrong obstinacy is added an itch for gain and a desire of "rising faster than the nature of the thing admitted." Rather than indicating the power of choice on Crusoe's part, these "decisions" thus mark the further enslavement of his will. When, for instance, he undertakes the slaving venture, he says "I was hurried on, and obeyed blindly the dictates of my fancy rather than my reason." By this time there really is an element of fatality in his actions, and his situation approaches that described by Tillotson in a sermon "Of the Deceitfulness and Danger of Sin": "when men have brought themselves to this pass, they are almost under a fatal necessity of sinning on. I do not believe that God hath absolutely predestinated any man to ruin, but by a long course of wilful sin men may in a sort predestinate themselves to it, and chuse wickedness so long till it almost becomes necessary, and till they have brought themselves under all imaginable disadvantage of contributing any thing towards their own recovery." The role of habit in hardening the sinner, and depriving him of the very power to see, much less choose, what is good, will be examined in more detail in the next chapter. Here the process is noted merely as another feature of Crusoe's wanderings that shows his worsening spiritual predicament.

A third and most important characteristic of these wanderings is that Crusoe neglects or actively flouts each opportunity to reverse his course. In addition to the relinquishment, first of rational choice, then gradually of any effective control over the course of events, his progress in sin is marked by a growing obtuseness towards Providential threats and deliverances. He goes on in his willful truancy despite invitations, both gentle and harsh, to mend his ways. The various natural phenomena that affect his outward career so drastically can be regarded as making up a regular series of such invitations, and indeed Crusoe himself comes to see them in this light at the time of his conversion.

That God brings about tempests, earthquakes, and other apparent deviations from the even tenor of things was a natural corollary of the doctrine of Providence; nor was it inconsistent with "scientific" explanation of meteors, eclipses, and epidemics to attribute them to God. Through a distinction between first and second causes, this belief managed to hold its own long after rational explanations were available, and the phenomena themselves had ceased to be objects of merely superstitious awe. Equally widespread and enduring was the belief that such phenomena, whatever their scientific explanations, are more or less explicit statements of God's intention towards those affected. With so many biblical precedents for the divine punishment of cities or nations, it is not surprising that the three major public calamities of Defoe's lifetime—the plague of 1665, the fire of 1666, and the storm of 1703—were generally interpreted as tokens of God's wrath towards English sins. But readers have often been disturbed by the extension of this doctrine to cases involving single individuals. The supposition that one man could provoke God to stir up the elements for his personal warning or correction has struck many critics as sheer fanaticism. As noted [elsewhere], nineteenth- and twentieth-century editors are consistently exasperated by what they regard as the grotesque self-importance of spiritual autobiographers in such circumstances, and critics of Defoe have been equally prompt to label this belief, expressed at various points in his works, one of his traits of residual Puritan enthusiasm.

But it did not seem so to Defoe's contemporaries. In the writings of Anglicans and Dissenters alike, man is exhorted to observe, interpret, and heed all such phenomena as declarations of the divine will. In any given storm or epidemic, the individual will be either one of the sufferers or one of those spared: in either case he is obliged to scrutinize the event for its significance to him personally. As afflictions, such events were often discussed in terms of the text, "Know ye the rod, and who hath appointed it" (Mic. 6:9). In a sermon delivered at Dr. Annesley's Cripplegate Exercises, the well-known Dissenter William Bates deplores the failure to do so as "a prodigious despising of God's hand"; and John Ryther imputes this fault more particularly to mariners who disregard storms. They are deaf, he says, to the calls of Providence: "God speaks to them once, yea twice, by his judgments as well as his mercies, but they regard him not. They are called upon to 'hear the voice of the rod, and him that hath appointed it,' but they are 'like the deaf adder'; nothing makes them hear or feel. Afflictions are lost upon them. The storm does not awaken them." In neglecting to read a meaning for himself in storms at sea, the sailor effectively frustrates the divine purpose in sending them. It is only gradually, however, that he acquires this callousness: at first he tends to be alarmed, and to form good resolutions, but after weathering a few storms his terror wears off, and boldness, or even bravado, takes its place. Preachers very frequently dwelt on this process because it furnished such a neat paradigm for the course of sinners in general. It appears not only in sermons addressed to seamen, where we should expect to find it, but as a commonplace of seventeenth-century religious literature. That Crusoe himself undergoes this process has been suggested earlier, and will be shown in more detail. Once again, motifs employed constantly in spiritual autobiographies and practical works for their illustrative or metaphorical value are woven into the actual, outward narrative of *Robinson Crusoe,* yet seem to retain their conventional significance.

A related point about Crusoe's afflictions arises from the very fact that they all have to do more or less directly with the sea. In stressing the idea that every calamity contains a Providential lesson for those affected by it, preachers often maintained that the specific nature of the visitation will suggest its import, though some link with what is amiss. In the words of one divine, "whatever particular proportion or correspondence you may observe between this or that circumstance in your affliction and your former transgressions, be especially careful to act according to that more peculiar and express voice of the rod." An interesting analogy was used to enforce this argument. Thomas Manton, an influential Dissenter, says that "When the sin is written upon the judgment, and there are some remarkable circumstances wherein the sin and the judgment meet . . . God's retaliation is very notable. Many judgments have a signature upon them, as many herbs in nature have a signature to show for what use they serve." Among Manton's Anglican contemporaries, John Tillotson uses the same image in a sermon on "The bad and the good Use of God's signal Judgments upon others": "the hand of God doth sometimes as it were by a finger point at the sin, which it designs to punish: as . . . when a sin is punish'd in its own kind, with a judgment so plainly suited to it, and so pat, that the punishment carries the very mark and signature of the sin upon it." Anglican and Dissenter thus agree that an event may, like an herb, bear outward marks of its meaning or function. This is noteworthy in itself, as further evidence of the tendency to regard all objects and events as having a significance, whether obvious or latent, which man must extract from them. But it has particular bearing on Crusoe's own afflictions. His main impulse in running away is towards the sea itself, rather than any ulterior economic or geographic goal; to him the sea is sufficient attraction, and not the route to any destination, or even the setting for any career. By the same token, the sea turns out to be more than the mere scene of his afflictions. The Captain of the ship that founders in Yarmouth Roads interprets Crusoe's first sea venture for him: " 'Young man,' says he, 'you ought never to go to sea any more, you ought to take this for a plain and visible token, that you are not to be a seafaring man.' " He goes on, in fact, to make quite explicit the comparison between Crusoe and Jonah. The result is that the sea, the very object of Crusoe's infatuation, becomes the providential agent of his chastisement. So it is especially revealing that the sea should prove so hostile to him: his tribulations seem to have "the very mark and signature" of his sins upon them, and his failure to grasp this at the time serves as a further indication of his blind willfulness.

In certain cases, of course, tempests and similar phenomena might operate as deliverances rather than afflictions. When a city or nation escapes a doom threatening to overwhelm it, or when an individual is spared the common effects of fire, plague, or other general calamities, Providence is again responsible. Indeed, afflictions and deliverances are regarded as having essentially the same purpose, so that sermons of humiliation and thanksgiving tend to be strikingly similar in argument if not in tone. In other words, God's dealings with man may vary outwardly, but they are uniform in intent. Two special features of providential deliverances should be noted, however. First there is the fact that deliverances at sea were seen as particularly dramatic and convincing instances of the role of Providence, so that these nautical motifs occur in religious works of all kinds. Following David's declaration in Psalm 107 that God's workings are remarkably clear in the case of those who "go down to the sea in ships, and occupy their business in great waters," preachers and poets alike drew heavily on seafaring for providential exempla. It is true that Newtonian astronomy supplied new illustrations of the extent of general Providence, ordering and sustaining the universe as a whole. But the benevolent operation of particular Providence continued to be shown through traditional images, such as these maritime ones. In his poem on Providence, for instance, John Pomfret says,

> Let the poor Ship-wreck'd Saylor show,
> To what invisible protecting Pow'r
>   He did his Life and Safety owe,
> When the loud Storm his well-built Vessel tore,
> And half a shatter'd Plank convey'd him to the Shore.

Passages similar to this one were quoted earlier; they are very common, and are mentioned here only to stress again that the intimate association between the doctrine of Providence and the incidents of seafaring occurs not only in homiletic and practical works, but is characteristic of imaginative literature in general at this period.

Another important feature of these providential deliverances is summed up in a text frequently preached upon, "Call upon me in the day of trouble, and I will deliver thee, and thou shalt glorify me" (Ps. 50:15). We have seen that afflictions, far from being the result of accident or chance, are brought about by God to reclaim sinners, and that deliverances have the same cause and purpose. But deliverances have the futher function of making man acknowledge his dependence on God for all goods. They demonstrate to him, in an especially forcible way, that not only his welfare, but his bare preservation, is a gift for which he should be thankful.

Bearing these ideas in mind, we may return to the problem of interpreting Crusoe's own career. From the time he first embarks at Hull, he undergoes a varied sequence of afflictions and deliverances; although each does contribute to the action by bringing him a step nearer the island, his "strange surprising adventures" are of a conventional kind, and help to chart the stages of his inward condition. That they have this latter function is indicated not only by the spiritual significance traditionally attached to such happenings, but more explicitly by Crusoe's own comments. Although he fully comprehends these events only after conversion, there are some guides to their meaning even as they take place: in the course of the storm off Yarmouth, he twice likens himself to the prodigal son, the Captain compares him to Jonah, and the action itself resembles the biblical stories at several points. By what I have called a kind of allusive shorthand, Defoe manages to suggest the spiritual connotations of Crusoe's actions. But other forms of explicit commentary are to be found prior to his conversion.

When he sets out from Brazil on his slaving venture, for instance, Crusoe carefully notes that "I went on board in an evil hour . . . being the same day eight year that I went from my father and mother at Hull, in order to act the rebel to their authority, and the fool to my own interest." Only after his conversion, to be sure, does he calculate in detail the "strange concurrence of days in the various providences that befell me," and the full significance of this phenomenon is elaborated only in the *Serious Reflections*. Yet even at this point in the narrative, although the modern reader is unlikely to share Defoe's attitude towards such coincidences, the very assertion of this link between the two embarkations suggests their substantive affinity; and since the spiritual implications of the first are already fairly clear, the reader is left in little doubt as to the meaning of the second. This, then, is another device by which Defoe is able to comment on the action and at the same time to establish thematic coherence between outwardly dissimilar episodes.

Nevertheless, the most effective commentary in this portion of the book probably is furnished not by what Crusoe says but precisely by what he fails to say. We have seen how divines of the period regarded such afflictions and deliverances, and how actual survivors of shipwrecks and escapees from slavery "improved" their experiences; indeed, we find Crusoe himself reflecting on these incidents after his conversion in the very manner that so many divines prescribed and so many seafarers practiced. The point is that at the time he undergoes them, they provoke no such reflections. He goes heedlessly on, at first unwilling and gradually unable to perceive the providential import of his vicissitudes. Their function in the book, then, is not merely to bring him plausibly to an island off the mouth of the Orinoco, but more basically to reveal his increasing obduracy and obtuseness.

I have spoken of several gradual processes in this portion of the book—gradual alienation from God, gradual loss of control over events, gradual hardening—and it is worth looking more closely at their progressive or cumulative character. What happens is that Crusoe reaches his lowest spiritual ebb not at the time of committing his "original sin" but just before conversion. It may seem paradoxical to maintain that he embodies a conventional progression in sin. What new sins does he commit? Is not his sense of sin (when it does emerge) in excess of the actual number and enormity of his misdeeds? Part of an answer to such questions has been suggested already: if he does not repeat his dramatic violation of the fifth commandment, or learn to break any of the latter five, he nevertheless does in effect flout the first more and more boldly. It is true, in other words, that he does not sin against the paternal or social order after first running away, but his defiance of divine order becomes a settled pattern of action. Writers on habitual sin maintained not only that one sin tends to lead to other and greater sins unless repentance intervenes, but also that failure to repent for a past sin is equivalent, in terms of the welfare of one's soul, to the actual commission of new sins. Thus even if each rejection of a providential call to conversion did not constitute a new sin, Crusoe's later sense of sinfulness would be justified by his prolonged failure to repent of the single, initial sin. In fact, however, he is culpable on both counts, for divines were emphatic in condemning what one of them calls "a daring contradiction to Providence, or a bold venturing on in sin, notwithstanding the vertual-wooings and warning-knocks of Providence to the contrary." The "bold venturing on" not only allows past sin to take firmer hold, but is sinful in itself, so that the guilt is compounded.

Turning to the actual details of this process in Crusoe's case, we may begin by recalling the resemblance to Balaam mentioned earlier. Like Crusoe, Balaam ventures forth on a mission contrary to his clear duty; like Crusoe, his way is opposed by God, but he is blind to the cause of the obstacles, and persists obstinately on his course. As with Crusoe, only the appearance of an angel, brandishing a sword and threatening his destruction, finally forces him to repent. What I wish to draw attention to here is not the outward similarity between, for instance, the two visions of armed, avenging angels, but the inward affinity between the spiritual plights of Balaam and Crusoe. In each case journeying bodily is a graphic representation of erring spiritually; in both cases the ways of sin are repeatedly obstructed, and ultimately blocked altogether, in order to deflect the culprit from his false object and restore him to the true path.

Various biblical and classical analogues to this process were available to preachers of the period. Obadiah Sedgwick says that God sometimes tries to reclaim erring man *"by a most perfect beleagring* (as it were) *of a projecting sinner:* hedging up all his ways with thorns, or immuring him as in a Castle, and shutting of him up, that there shall be no going out or coming in." Seen in these terms, Crusoe's arrival on the island marks yet another more drastic stage in God's efforts to reclaim him. It is at once the most dramatic of his long series of deliverances, and the most effective barrier to his persistent vagabondage. The shipwreck is meant to halt his erring career and to awaken him to a new life; what happens, however, is that only his outward circumstances change. Initially, to be sure, he is struck by his escape, but his elation soon gives way to despair, for, as he records in his journal, "instead of being thankful to God for my deliverance . . . I ran about the shore, wringing my hands, and beating my head and face, exclaiming at my misery, and crying out, I was undone, undone." When he does regain his composure, he once again fails to interpret the personal significance of what he has just experienced.

On the one hand, the brief ecstasy, as he later calls it, "ended where it began, in a mere common flight of joy," without leading to any "reflection upon the distinguished goodness of the hand which had preserved me," or any "inquiry why Providence had been thus merciful to me." On the other hand, he later acknowledges that as soon as he saw he was not doomed to starve, "all the sense of my affliction wore off . . . [I] was far enough from being afflicted at my condition, as a judgment from heaven, or as the hand of God against me." Regarded *either* as a deliverance or as an affliction, this episode might have taken effect, but in fact the Providential design in it is frustrated, and it takes its place among the calls to repentance which go unheeded. In terms of Crusoe's spiritual state, it marks yet another slight of the "vertual-wooings and warning-knocks of Providence"; like Balaam, he goes mulishly on, although "by a most perfect beleagring (as it were)" the way of the "projecting sinner" is now hedged up with thorns. Thus the arrival at the island may be less of a turning point than is generally supposed: a new beginning in only a qualified sense, it is more basically an extension of a pattern of action initiated by the embarkation at Hull.

Two important episodes between Crusoe's landing on the island and his conversion are discussed in the Appendix—namely the springing up of the barley, and the earthquake. In light of the foregoing discussion, it should be clear why Crusoe later singles out these two incidents, among all those between his landing and his sickness, for special regretful comment. Like the events just considered, they again display Providence's concern for him and power over him; they again invite him (once gently, once harshly) to repent; but they again fail to take effect. Rather than dwelling further here on their significance, we shall find it more fruitful to turn directly to the climactic episode of this long series: Crusoe's illness.

It was of course traditional to represent spiritual infirmity through bodily disease, to express God's cure of souls in medical metaphors, and to regard actual sickness as a particularly opportune occasion for setting repentance in motion. Seen against such a background, Crusoe's malady is another striking instance of Defoe's ability to exploit fully the narrative possibilities of commonplace events, and at the same time to avail himself of their conventional spiritual significance. Thus the chart of Crusoe's case history, which he is made to record in his journal, has a thoroughly clinical verisimilitude; this gives the dream and its consequences a plausibility which they might have lacked had they come, for instance, in a season of callous, bustling prosperity. More fundamentally, however, Crusoe's sickness and dream serve as final indications of the spiritual condition which he has reached, and of the greatness of the change he is about to undergo. These effects are achieved partly, as already noted, by the overt resemblance between this stern apparition and certain biblical ones. But they are also owing in part to the tradition of hardy sinners bowed by sickness. Without recapitulating earlier discussion of such motifs in spiritual autobiographies, or citing any further evidence of their prevalence in homiletic and practical works, we may recall that they appear very early in the literature of conversion. As one of Defoe's contemporaries obligingly pointed out to his parishioners, "not only by outward Means, but by immediate Operations and Impressions, and those, very sensible, strong, and lively, have the Convictions of some Men been wrought in them. Of all which, St. *Austin* is a most remarkable Instance, who in his *Confessions* (a Book I think translated into English and worthy your Perusal) hath recorded the many Warnings he had from God, by his own Sickness; the Death of his Companions in Sin; the overruling Providences of God; the inward Motions, and Convictions of his own Conscience; and at last by a *Voice* from Heaven; commanding him to take up the Bible, and read."

The preceding examination of Crusoe's adventures after embarking at Hull has shown that besides merely leading him to the island by plausible stages, they function as "the many Warnings" which he, like Augustine, "had from God," and that their sequence is completed not with the arrival at the island but at the point of conversion. The fact that nothing less drastic than the appearance of an avenging angel will serve to awaken Crusoe indicates how grave his spiritual malady has become, yet at the same time enhances the importance of his conversion and heightens the attainments possible to him through regeneration. Earlier chapters have discussed the trait, so common to spiritual autobiographers, of magnifying one's ultimate condition by contrasting it with what preceded conversion. Regarded in these terms, Crusoe's vicissitudes magnify the scope, the patience, and the benevolence of Providence; his conversion, however, magnifies not only the abundance of grace to the sinner, but also, by implication, the potential stature of the ex-sinner himself. It was said of the Puritan worthy Robert Bolton that "it pleased God to bring him to repentance, but by such a way as the Lord seldom useth, but upon such strong vessels, as he intendeth for strong encounters, and rare employments; for the Lord ranne upon him as a Giant, taking him by the neck, and shaking him to pieces, as he did *Iob;* beating him to the ground as he did *Paul,* by laying before him the ugly visage of his sins, which lay so heavy upon him that he roared for anguish of heart." It is in this tradition that Defoe places Crusoe, by investing his conversion with such grand agents as a fire-clad, spear-brandishing apparition. The section that follows will examine the conversion itself, and Crusoe's subsequent fortunes, in order to establish whether, and in what sense, he is a strong vessel intended for strong encounters and rare employments.

CONVERSION AND REGENERATION

In one of his essays, Lord Clarendon says of repentance that "It is almost the only point of faith upon which there is no controversy." Moreover the concept was a fairly simple one, definable in a sentence or two. But despite the clear and uncontroversial nature of the doctrine, the process by which one actually came to repent might be quite complex: in fact, there was a regular progression through which autobiographers and other writers on repentance usually led their readers. First there was the provocation to repentance—the event or impression which set the whole process in motion; next there was reflection or consideration, a "coming to oneself"; this was followed by "conviction" or "godly sorrow," a phase of remorseful self-accusation; then there came the stage, to which most writers reserved the term "conversion," when God actually relieved and reclaimed the sufferer. Each of the stages could vary considerably in form and intensity, but their sequence was fairly constant, and we find Crusoe passing through them in the traditional manner.

At the end of the preceding section it was noted that the vision of the avenging angel which precipitates Crusoe's repentance, however fanciful it may seem, his various precedents. As one of Bishop Hall's *Soliloquies,* on "God's Various Proceedings," points out, the ways of initiating the process are infinite:

"What strange varieties do I find in the workings of God with man! one, where I find him gently and plausibly inviting men to their conversion; another, where I find him frighting some others to heaven: some, he trains up in a goodly education, and, without any eminent change, calls them forth to an exemplary profession of his name; some others, he chooseth out of a life notoriously lewd to be the great patterns of a sudden reformation: one, that was only formal in his devotion, without any true life of grace, is, upon a grievous sickness, brought to a lively sense of godliness; . . . another, that was cast down with a sad despair of God's mercy, is raised up by the fall of an unbroken glass, or by some comfortable dream, or by the seasonable word of a cheerful friend: one is called at the sixth hour; another, not till the eleventh: one, by fair and probable means; another, by contraries; so as even the work of Satan himself hath been made the occasion of the conversion of his soul."

In Crusoe's case it is a dream, but scarcely a "comfortable" one, that effectually bestirs him. Unlike his previous alarms, which had soon subsided, this one provokes him to review his past career: "conscience," he says, "that had slept so long, began to awake, and I began to reproach myself with my past life." He now reflects on the various Providential chastisements and deliverances which he had neglected or dismissed. In doing so, he becomes keenly aware of his spiritual plight, and thus moves a step closer to repentance. His reflections at this stage make up what writers on the subject generally refer to as "consideration"; this typically merges into "conviction," and such is the case with Crusoe. He reports that amid the "dreadful reproaches of my conscience, . . . My thoughts were confused, the convictions great upon my mind, and the horror of dying in such a miserable condition, raised vapours into my head with the mere apprehensions." Such sorrows and fears commonly mark this phase of the process, for, as one writer observes, "The work of Regeneration or the New Birth cannot be wrought without many pangs or throwes, nor does God ever almost bring a bad man to become a good one without some trouble and disorder of Mind." Indeed, Crusoe's state borders on despair; his oppressive reflections, he says, "extorted some words from me, like praying to God, though I cannot say they were either a prayer attended with desires or with hopes; it was rather the voice of mere fright and distress." And in the depths of his depression he finds himself facing "difficulties to struggle with, too great for even Nature itself to support, and no assistance, no help, no comfort, no advice." Our analyses of Fraser's *Memoirs* and the *Account* have shown how the opening phases of repentance tend to reduce the penitent to a low ebb of despondency, in which he feels altogether helpless and abandoned; only when he has acknowledged his own utter insufficiency and worthlessness is he in a posture to receive forgiveness and relief. This also is true of Crusoe. Having voiced the lament just quoted, he cries out, "Lord, be my help, for I am in great distress." This, "the first prayer, if I may call it so, that I had made for many years," signals the submission which the long series of vicissitudes considered in the preceding section had been designed, but had failed, to bring about.

Crusoe's "convictions," however, do not in themselves constitute repentance, for although godly sorrow was seen as an essential stage or component of repentance, it makes up only a part of the total process. As shown earlier, it was believed that once man had been brought to contrite humility, God had to interpose if the matter was not to end in total despair. Actual conversion, in other words, was regarded as a gift which man can and must make himself eligible to receive, but which he cannot command or obtain by his own efforts. Crusoe's convictions, culminating in his first brief prayer, render him fit for the help he implores; as with the father in the parable, God's grace goes out to meet and reclaim the returning prodigal. It is interesting to observe that Defoe employs external detail, at this point as elsewhere, to indicate the inward spiritual state of the hero. Just as grave bodily illness parallels the crisis in Crusoe's spiritual malady, so the first stirrings of spiritual renewal are heralded by the signs of physical recovery that appear the day after his prayer. It seems significant that the sea, too, which has hitherto proved such a consistently hostile and turbulent element in his experience, is on this occasion "very calm and smooth." In any case Crusoe, who is still too weak to walk, sits down on the ground, gazes out to sea, and meditates, with the insight of a fledgling physico-theologist, on the significance of what he sees. Though he lacks as yet the aid of God's Word, he now begins to perceive God through his Works. The implication is that unless one is willfully blind—as indeed Crusoe has been up to this point—it quickly becomes obvious that "God has made all these things," and that "He guides and governs them all," as well, so that "nothing can happen in the great circuit of His works, either without His knowledge or appointment." Crusoe's dawning awareness that all creation, including himself, is subject to the disposition of Providence still does not afford him consolation, however: at this point it merely deepens his sense of folly and guilt in having been so long oblivious of the fact. But such an acknowledgment of God's power, coinciding with Crusoe's bodily weakness in the first stage of convalescence, opens the way to divine relief. Thus "directed by Heaven no doubt," he rummages in one of the salvaged sea-chests, where he finds the Bible and some tobacco, "a cure both for soul and body." Opening the Bible, he reads as the first words those of Psalm 50, "Call upon me in the day of trouble, and I will deliver thee, and thou shalt glorify me." His first response, it is true, is to interpret deliverance as referring to his isolation; of deliverance in this sense, the prospect is so faint that he forms no great hopes. But it soon occurs to him that in poring so much upon deliverance "from the main affliction," he is disregarding the deliverance from sickness he has just received, and before long it further dawns on him that according to "a true sense of things," one "will find deliverance from sin a much greater blessing than deliverance from affliction."

He does not gain this latter realization, however, until after a second encounter with an apposite biblical text:

> I was earnestly begging of God to give me repentance, when it happened providentially, the very day, that reading the Scripture, I came to these words, "he is exalted a Prince and a Saviour, to give repentance, and to give remission" [Defoe's paraphrase of Acts 5:31]. I threw down the book; and with my heart as well as my hands lifted up to heaven, in a kind of ecstasy of joy, I cried aloud, "Jesus . . . Thou exalted Prince and Saviour, give me repentance!"

This was the first time that I could say, in the true sense of the words, that I prayed in all my life; for now I prayed with a sense of my condition, and with a true Scripture view of hope founded on the encouragement of the Word of God; and from this time, I may say, I began to have hope that God would hear me.

If any single episode can be isolated as the book's turning point, it is probably this one. God's threats give way to his promises, and Crusoe's dismal apprehensions are replaced by a hope that grows towards assurance.

Yet it is worth observing that this change, significant as it is, is presented with a minimum of rapture, nor is there any pretense to total, immediate transformation. The reasons for this have already been suggested: reacting in embarrassment against the enthusiastic transports of earlier conversion accounts, spiritual autobiographers of the late seventeenth and early eighteenth centuries tried to avoid the stigma of fanaticism by speaking of the change with careful restraint, by repressing any tendency to revel garrulously in their newfound grace. Thus Crusoe does momentarily experience "a kind of ecstacy of joy," but does not dwell on these emotions; nor to be sure is this elation lasting, although, as Fraser had quietly remarked, "something remained." Moreover, his regeneration is by no means instantaneous. Like the recovery from his ague, it is a gradual regaining of strength. What has come upon him with suddenness is the grace to repent and the hope of obtaining remission of his sins: the actual work of regeneration is achieved only through a settled change in attitude and behavior, and clearly requires time.

Although this conversion scene is remarkably free from cant about either the sensations or the extent of the change, Defoe nevertheless makes clear that a change of great significance has taken place. Crusoe reflects almost at once that "My condition now began to be, though not less miserable as to my way of living, yet much easier to my mind . . . I had a great deal of comfort within, which, till now, I knew nothing of." In fact, the attainment of a new kind and degree of serenity is one of the most marked characteristics of his latter state. This is not to say, of course, that he is now simply freed from all anxiety. At various points in the subsequent narrative he experiences "frights" and "consternations"; some of them are fully as harrowing as the "strange surprising adventures" that preceded his conversion, and perhaps more so, since he had then been callous towards dangers and deliverances alike. Now, however, he becomes better able to confront new hazards, and to dispel their terrors, for he gains security from the conviction that he is an object of Providential care. In other words, it is not that his belief shields him from further vicissitudes, but that such vicissitudes either fail to discompose him or else agitate him only when he forgets he is under divine protection.

Evidence of this is to be found in Crusoe's discovery of the footprint in the sand. We are given a lively picture of his terrors, both on the beach and during the sleepless night that follows. After recounting them at great length, he confesses "Thus my fear banished all my religious hope. All that former confidence in God, which was founded upon such wonderful experience as I had had of His goodness, now vanished, as if He that had fed me by miracle hitherto could not preserve, by His power, the provision which He had made for me by His goodness." But afterward, "when [he] had a little recovered [his] first suprise," Crusoe again calls to mind the power, wisdom, and bounty or Providence, and thus regains his composure. He reflects that " 'twas my unquestioned duty to resign myself absolutely and entirely to His will; and, on the other hand, it was my duty also to hope in Him, pray to Him, and quietly to attend the dictates and directions of His daily Providence." And again, when his "cogitations, apprehensions, and reflections" return to disturb him, he recalls the passage from Psalm 50 which had been of such service to him during his sickness, and declares, "Upon this, rising cheerfully out of my bed, my heart was not only comforted, but I was guided and encouraged to pray earnestly to God for deliverance. When I had done praying, I took up my Bible, and opening it to read, the first words that presented to me were, 'Wait on the Lord, and be of good cheer, and He shall strengthen thy heart; wait, I say, on the Lord.' It is impossible to express the comfort this gave me. In answer, I thankfully laid down the book, and was no more sad, at least, not on that occasion."

At other times, too, Crusoe is downcast: his trust in Providence does not exempt him from alarms and dejections, but it reasserts itself so as to rescue him from them. Conversion was not seen as providing immunity to spiritual turmoils, but rather a new strength with which to resolve them, and it is this that Crusoe gains.

Whatever its interruptions, then, his attitude becomes one of composure; this composure springs from a mixture of hope and resignation, which in turn is owing to a new awareness of the existence and nature of Providence. His new attitude not only supports him in the various crises which punctuate his later years on the island, as I have just argued, but also largely offsets the painful loneliness of his long isolation. One of the early results of his repentance is that, as he puts it, "I acquiesced in the dispositions of Providence, which I began now to own and to believe ordered everything for the best." Through such acquiescence, he learns to find both consolations for and positive benefits in his solitary state. This aspect of his situation is expressed most forcibly in his series of annual thanksgivings, but it appears on other occasions as well. Indeed, it was a constant theme in preaching of the period that solitude has special compensations for those who realize that they are never out of the presence of God. Thus Edward Waple, drawing on Cicero's *Offices,* argues that as follows: "If a wise Heathen could say, that he was never less idle than when he was out of Business; nor less alone than when he was in Private; . . . How much more can a Christian say so, who believes one Supreme God, and a Providence, and invisible Powers above him, and can look up to Heaven, with Confidence to God, as a Father in Christ; and can lay all his Wants, and his Necessities before him, in assurance of being heard, and relieved by him. O comfortable Retirement! O happy Rest! or may I not rather say, O *blessed Company, O busy* and *laborious Rest!"* Crusoe's reactions to his solitude do vary, of course, so that he lapses more than once into extreme melancholy over his condition. Yet on the whole his isolation is made tolerable, and frequently strikes him as a positive blessing. Recognizing his dependence on Providence, he submits to its government and becomes responsive to manifestations of its will concerning him. But its very immediacy is as important to his peace of mind as its power and beneficence, since it is a sense of God's nearness and accessibility that supplies his *"blessed Company."*

Nor is his regeneration confined to the change in belief or attitude. Though the inward alteration is basic, his overt behavior is equally affected, and offers palpable evidence of the change that has taken place within him. In the first place, certain habitual or at least recurrent actions bespeak his altered condition. Hopeful resignation has already been mentioned as a feature of his inward change; it finds tangible expression, however, in his prayers and thanksgivings. Surveys of his activities which take into account all that he builds and grows, all his carpentry and husbandry, his potting and baking, but omit or slight these religious observances, are at best incomplete and at worst seriously distorted. Not only do the latter bulk large in the narrative, but they give the economic activity itself a meaning which it had lacked prior to conversion. As is demonstrated more fully in the Appendix, Crusoe now goes about his tasks in a different spirit, so that both the objects and the results of his labors are conditioned by his prayers and thanksgivings. Through prayer, he seeks and obtains divine guidance and assistance in his efforts; and through ascribing their outcome to Providence, he not only takes new relish in those which succeed, but manages to be undismayed by those which are delayed, botched, or frustrated.

Other practices as well reflect the spiritual transformation that Crusoe undergoes. Although he comes to acquiesce in what Providence determines as his lot, and to depend upon divine support and protection, he is by no means passive; he learns to recognize and heed its warnings and promptings. This attitude leads to what some critics have regarded as a superstitious concern for hints and portents, but within the traditions of belief already discussed, Crusoe's keen attention to apparent trivia is not excessive. In a world in which nothing can occur without providential design, piety alone obliges man to vigilance, and since Providence concerns itself in a direct, personal way with the welfare of the individual, prudence likewise demands watchfulness. An earlier chapter has argued that this double incentive is largely responsible for the thoroughness with which spiritual autobiographers assessed everything that happened to them: besides obtaining indications of their spiritual condition, they were thus able to satisfy the twin dictates of thankfulness and circumspection.

It is particularly noteworthy that Crusoe should come to act in this way, for it provides a fundamental contrast with his earlier behavior. His initial disobedience, as we have seen, had been both sinful and rash. Now, however, through attending, interpreting, and obeying various manifestations of the divine will towards him, he attains the corresponding virtues of piety and prudence. An example is his reaction to visitors from the outside world, the cannibals and the English crew. On each occasion he is restrained, by secret doubts or admonitions, from encounters that would have been his undoing; in both cases he pauses to advise "all considering men, whose lives are attended with such extraordinary incidents as mine, or even though not so extraordinary, not to slight such secret intimations of

Providence. . . . Let no man despise the secret hints and notices of danger which sometimes are given him when he may think there is no possibility of its being real." In keeping, then, with the autobiographical conventions discussed earlier, Crusoe has frequent opportunities to ascribe his own preservation to Providence. But in addition, he becomes the agent of Providence in the salvation of others. This role is made quite explicit in the case of the English captain, and is an important motif in his dealings with Friday. The point here, however, is that Crusoe's regeneration involves not merely a change in attitude or belief, since his new outlook does affect his actual behavior. If for this reason alone, it seems a mistake to suppose that his religion amounts to no more than a superimposed and dispensable commentary on the action.

Crusoe's relations with Friday deserve particular attention because they supply yet another test of the importance of religious concerns to the book's total structure. Like the running away to sea and various events that follow, Friday's role has been discussed by one recent critic mainly in economic terms. His rescue merely marks "the advent of new manpower"; Crusoe's dealings with him are altogether egocentric; communication between them is strictly utilitarian, so that "A functional silence, broken only by an occasional 'No, Friday,' or an abject 'Yes, Master,' is the golden music of Crusoe's *île joyeuse*."

While it cannot be denied that Friday's arrival results in new planting and building, it is surely an error to regard this as its sole, or even its main implication. We have seen that a constant feature of spiritual autobiographies, and indeed a primary motive in their very composition, is the urge to impart to others the benefits of one's own conversion; we have also noted that the growth of this didactic impulse is a phenomenon recognized and endorsed by writers on regeneration other than autobiographers. On the one hand, to have experienced conversion oneself was regarded as a necessary qualification for evangelizing, and on the other, it was felt that genuine conversion naturally gives rise to a kind of missionary zeal. It is this aspect of Crusoe's relations with Friday that seems most striking, for after being "called plainly by Providence to save this poor creature's life," Crusoe becomes the Providential agent of his rescue from paganism.

Just as Crusoe had discovered for himself the essentials of Christianity by reading the Bible, contemplating the works of nature, and reflecting on his own experience, so his indoctrination of Friday provides a second demonstration of the simplicity and reasonableness of such belief as is necessary to salvation. Moreover, his guidance of Friday displays the progress of Crusoe's own regeneration, in that he now learns to expound and defend his faith. It is true that he is posed by several of Friday's ingenuous questions, and he acknowledges that "I was but a young doctor, and ill enough qualified for a casuist, or a solver of difficulties. . . . I had, God knows, more sincerity than knowledge in all the methods I took for this poor creature's instruction." But this confession, too, besides lending plausibility in the same way as do his awkward improvisations in other spheres, is part of the traditional conception of the fledgling spiritual guide. As was shown earlier, the lay convert was encouraged to share his discoveries with others not only for the good it might do them but for the value it must have to himself. [Elsewhere] we saw the double function—didactic and autodidactic—ascribed throughout the period to spiritual autobiography in particular, and to the exchange of religious knowledge and experience in general. Here the principle is made quite explicit, in Crusoe's declaration that "in laying things open to him, I really informed and instructed myself in many things that either I did not know, or had not fully considered before, but which occurred naturally to my mind upon my searching into them for the information of this poor savage. And I had more affection in my inquiry after things upon this occasion than ever I felt before; so that whether this poor wild wretch was the better for me or no, I had great reason to be thankful that ever he came to me." In short, communication between Crusoe and Friday is "utilitarian" in a sense quite different from that which Mr. Watt has in mind. It is useful not to one party but to both, and it is useful not so much for the exploitation of new manpower—signs, effective enough at first, would have remained sufficient for that—as for the salvation of one soul and the growth of another.

Besides becoming Friday's spiritual mentor, Crusoe is also his master, and a further point should be made about this aspect of their relationship. Prior to his conversion, Crusoe rebels against divine authority, yet his attempt to become independent results in an actual loss of mastery over himself and his circumstances. Eventually, through submitting to God and acknowledging his dependence upon Providence, he in fact acquires a new degree of control over his environment, and over himself as well. In seeking to be a law unto himself, he had lost the power that was properly his; in surrendering to the sovereignty of Providence, he gains extraordinary powers. In any case, it seems legitimate to regard his mastery over Friday in this light, as made possible by his own submission to God, and as a further embodiment of a paradox running throughout the book: that sinful independence results in Crusoe's enslavement, both literal and figurative, while virtuous dependence issues in mastery, again literal and figurative.

The paradox might also be stated in terms of the relation between parent and child. In the early part of the book Crusoe virtually orphans himself through disobedience: in challenging the authority of a father he loses the security of a son. But through humbling himself towards his other Father, and reassuming the dutifulness of a son, Crusoe paradoxically gains parental power himself, since his relations with Friday are in large part those of father to child, as he himself declares. Thus the parent-child motif further illustrates the nature and extent of the change that Crusoe undergoes.

Crusoe's encounters with Friday and the other savages raise another interesting issue, which was to be treated fully in the *Serious Reflections,* in chapters on "The Present State of Religion in the World" and "Of the Proportion between the Christian and Pagan World." Crusoe asks himself "why it has pleased God to hide . . . saving knowledge from so many millions of souls, who, if I might judge by this poor savage, would make a much better use of it than we did." This problem perplexed Europe throughout the period, and was to have profound effects on Christian thinking, as explorers continued to bring back reports of heathen races in remote lands. It is worth observing, however, that in *Robinson Crusoe* the question is subsumed in the more pervasive issue of the hero's own relationship to God. What happens is that Crusoe's musings on the matter lead him, as he confesses, "too far to invade the sovereignty of Providence, and as it were arraign the justice of so arbitrary a disposition of things"; ultimately the question is not so much resolved by any direct answer as dismissed by a gesture of humble acquiescence on the part of the questioner. It is all very well to be concerned about the fate of "millions of souls," but it is still more important not to jeopardize one's own by questioning, much less challenging, the providential "disposition of things." It is not that Defoe lacked answers: he had them, as he was to prove abundantly in the *Serious Reflections*. It is rather that Crusoe's responses to the problem—first

presumptuous, then proper—are what really matter. Once again
Defoe has inserted in the narrative an issue possessing intrinsic interest and importance, which would be explored for its own sake in
his other writings but which, in the setting of *Robinson Crusoe,* is
subordinated to a primary concern with the spiritual development of
the hero.

Crusoe's relationship with Friday can be summed up in this
way: without denying that Friday's arrival has economic implications, it has other results which are equally prominent in purely
narrative terms, and probably more significant in thematic terms.
Nor is it merely a matter of Crusoe "carrying on a little missionary
activity as a sideline," as Basil Willey maintains. Far from being a
sideline, such activity is a crucial feature of Crusoe's regeneration: it
embodies the didactic impulse traditionally stimulated by conversion, and in its autodidactic aspect strengthens and extends the im-
pact of conversion on Crusoe himself. In short it bears out, at least
as dramatically as his celebrated triumphs in pottery and bakery, the
impression created by the events leading up to his conversion: that he
is a strong vessel whom the Lord "intendeth for strong encounters,
and rare employments."

Robinson Crusoe's Rebellion and Punishment

J. Paul Hunter

"To hear of a Man's living so long alone in a desert Island, seems to some very surprizing," writes Edward Cooke in 1712 about Alexander Selkirk, "and they presently conclude he may afford a very agreeable Relation of his Life, when in Reality it is the most barren Subject that Nature can afford." Cooke's own account of Selkirk seems to prove his point and similar accounts by Sir Richard Steele and Woodes Rogers hardly suggest that the subject is pregnant with artistic possibility. *Providence Displayed* and similar stories in providence books are somewhat more pointed, for they structure events according to a specific philosophy of history, but these accounts still fail to rise above the level of exemplum or polemical anecdote. Since 1719, hundreds of books have recounted stories with a similar setting and plot, employing the most highly praised features of *Robinson Crusoe,* but they also have failed to achieve lasting renown. Cooke's point would seem sound indeed, were it not for Defoe.

At first glance, *Robinson Crusoe* seems to disprove Cooke. Defoe turns the kind of plot Cooke describes into one of the most popular books of all time, but a closer examination suggests that Cooke is not so far wrong, for Defoe's achievement does not rest primarily on his having found a story with inherent mythic appeal. Critics who attribute *Robinson Crusoe*'s appeal to setting and plot have slipped into the fallacy which Cooke describes: the confusion of vehicle with

From *The Reluctant Pilgrim: Defoe's Emblematic Method and Quest for Form in* Robinson Crusoe. ©1966 by the Johns Hopkins University Press, Baltimore/London.

tenor, the failure to consider the effects of artistic rendering and, ultimately, the failure to consider artistic intent. What Defoe distills from desert island experience is not an "agreeable Relation" at all, but rather a rigorous multilevel moral examination of life, for the narrative is structured to render dimensions which are absent in stories of similar plot. Unlike its analogues, *Robinson Crusoe* derives dramatic power from its understanding of man's struggle against nature as both physical and metaphysical. Reared upon Puritan religious tradition and Puritan habits of mind, Defoe views Crusoe's struggles for survival against a background of established metaphors for existence and spiritual alienation, and he creates a world in which man's basic conflicts take place in a personal, physical setting with cosmic, spiritual significance. Although Milton and Bunyan are usually considered to present the poetry and prose epitomes of the Puritan view of life (and Defoe is thought to present only a fractured, diluted, and ultimately materialistic view of it), *Robinson Crusoe* also embodies the Puritan view of man on a most profound level; it also portrays, through the struggles of one man, the rebellion and punishment, repentance and deliverance, of all men, as they sojourn in a hostile world.

The island section is ultimately the most crucial part of *Robinson Crusoe*, not because of its sheer bulk or because the adventurous episodes on the island are more "exciting" than pre-island or post-island episodes, but because Defoe uses the island setting to isolate and resolve conflicts within Crusoe—conflicts that Crusoe shares with men in all places and all times. The simplified context of the island turns Crusoe's attention inward and forces him to look at the pattern of his life, to question the cause of his exile from civilization, and to examine the warring factions in his own nature. Defoe also uses the simplified context to alert the reader to the relationship between different levels of conflicts: man with God, man with nature, man with man, and man with himself.

On the island the movement of Crusoe's life—and the movement of the novel—is reversed. Travel, which means only flight to the young Crusoe, is transformed into pilgrimage, for Crusoe's conversion introduces purpose to his wanderings and informs his actions with real meaning. The island is a fitting climax to Crusoe's early aimlessness, but at the same time its confinement provides him with a new pace which is more conducive to reflection and redemption. The island, then, represents both punishment and potential salvation. What Crusoe thinks about on the island—and what he does—pivots the novel from a story about punishment to a story about deliverance, from a story about God's judgment to a story about God's mercy.

Before Crusoe's island struggles can be meaningful, however, Defoe must first define the nature of man's predicament by suggesting his depravity and weakness. Crusoe's pre-island adventures dramatize the attraction which evil holds for weak men, just as Crusoe's post-island adventures demonstrate the power which man may exert over his environment, his fellow man, and himself, after he has achieved a proper relationship with his God. Crusoe's rhythm of life is finely calculated, and Defoe manages to suggest that the rhythm is a matter of divine calculation, not simply of human artistry. But while artfully manipulating character and event to suggest an artless recording of divinely planned reality, Defoe gradually reveals Crusoe as a carefully wrought fictive creation. By judicious selection of events that dramatize Crusoe's personality and by careful manipulation of time and point of view to show Crusoe's developing awareness of himself and his world, Defoe delineates a man of striking individuality. By employing standard Puritan metaphors and by controlling a series of allusions, Defoe defines Crusoe as a kind of Everyman whose life and thought follow a pattern typical of man's voyage through life.

"We drive our selves away from the Port, at which we would arrive," says Bishop Patrick, "by these Storms and blustering Passions. If we would be carried to the Haven we desire, let us be calm and of a still and quiet Disposition." Crusoe's inability to control his irrational inclination to roam leads to his rejection of the ordered way of life recommended by his rational father and turns his course toward the *"Island of Despair."* The whole dialectic of decline and recovery in *Robinson Crusoe* results from the tension between human reason and Crusoe's "Propension of Nature," an antithesis that resembles Paul's spirit-flesh tension more than it does the reason-passion conflict often described by critics of the "Age of Reason." Like Pauline man, Crusoe finds himself the victim of his natural propensity to evil: he is unable to choose the right course even when aware of it. "I was hurried on," he says about his decision to leave Brazil and return to sea, "and obey'd blindly the Dictates of my Fancy rather than my Reason." His "Reason," although aided by the counsel of his elders and by supernatural warnings sent by providence, is still unable to overcome what seems to be "something fatal in that Propension of Nature tending directly to [a] Life of Misery." Crusoe finds himself incapable not only of controlling his will but even of understanding his incapacity, and he can only interpret mythically: "I had several times loud Calls from my Reason and my more composed Judgment to go home," he says after his first voyage, "yet I had no Power to do it. I know not what to call this, nor will I urge, that it is a secret overruling Decree that hurries us on to be the Instruments of our own Destruction, even tho' it be before us, and that we rush upon it with our Eyes open." Crusoe considers himself "born to be my own Destroyer" and thinks it "no great Wonder" "for me to do wrong that never did right." Throughout the early part of the novel, while his spiritual and physical fortunes are in decline, Crusoe remains powerless to deal with his "fatal" propensity to evil.

Crusoe's inner tension between reason and natural propensity ultimately reflects the war between good and evil. Crusoe's life, like that of all other men, is simply a battleground on which one phase of a general struggle takes place. Like any postlapsarian man, Crusoe finds the battle uneven as long as he depends solely upon his own resources; he cannot even grasp the grace proffered him until God specifically interposes. Until then, he may in theory choose on the side of good, for he has (according to seventeenth- and eighteenth-century Calvinist thought) free will, but in practice the result is inevitable: man is the victim of his depraved nature until God intervenes to free him.

"The effect of [Adam's] sin," Defoe writes in the 1715 volume of *The Family Instructor,* "is a corrupt and Taint which we all bring into the World with us, and which we find upon our Nature, by which we find a Natural Propensity to us to do Evil, and no natural Inclination to do Good." This concept of man's depravity is implicit in *Robinson Crusoe* and is fundamental to an understanding of Crusoe's actions. Natural man is not the "noble savage" pictured by some of Defoe's contemporaries. Because he is made in God's image, he has innate potentiality for good, but this potentiality can be realized only when God intervenes to save him from his fallen nature. Defoe's natural men, including Friday and his father, are savage cannibals in their ordinary state, and Defoe vividly dramatizes the horrors of their natural depravity. God interposes to convert Friday and uses Crusoe as his instrument—first, to rescue Friday from physical death, and later, to implant the Christian doctrine of salvation. (Defoe leaves Friday's father an unconverted cannibal and thus retains a dramatic touchstone of man's potential savagery in his natural, unregenerated state.) In a similar way Crusoe, although he has had the advantage of being reared by a "wise and grave" father in a presumably Christian setting, is also guided by his natural propensities in his early life. God has not yet interposed, and Crusoe lacks the conversion experience that he must have in order to gain control over his nature.

Defoe traces Crusoe's depravity along lines sketched by contemporary Puritan theology; he gives Crusoe a *dilectum delictum* (or "commanding sin") which rules his life and leads him into the straits from which he needs deliverance. According to writers in the guide tradition, man's depravity usually took a specific form in a particular individual, and the form determined the kind of sinful course the individual would follow. The idea of a dilectum delictum apparently derives from the patristic concept of *peccatum in deliciis* (the ultimate source, too, of the "ruling passion" idea upon which Pope draws in the *Essay of Man*), but guide writers reduced it to more simple terms (darling-pleasure, minion-delight, bosom-devil, captain sin, darling corruption) and argued that the entire force of man's natural depravity was often focused in this one sin. Crusoe's dilectum delictum is a form of the most basic human sins, a restlessness of body and mind which leads to discontent with one's station. It was this sin which caused man's original fall, and Puritan moralists regarded it as man's first and worst enemy. It was this sin which Herbert found basic, but ultimately self-redemptive, in "The Pulley." It was this sin to which the concept of the calling tried to minister.

Crusoe's tendency toward restlessness leads to what he describes as his "Original Sin" of leaving his station. He is inexplicably "hurried" into "the wild and indigested Notion of raising my Fortune"— a notion which, in context, suggests violation of God's order rather than accrual of material wealth. Later, when Crusoe begins to attain a stable life in Brazil, his restlessness returns: "increasing in Business and in Wealth," he reports, "my Head began to be full of Projects and Undertakings beyond my Reach." His "aspiring Thoughts," Crusoe decides in retrospect, are responsible for his "Ruin," a term which ultimately suggests not only his material but moral and spiritual bankruptcy. Lured by specific "Snares" laid by the devil ("Allurement[s] of Seafaring Men," companions who "entic'd me away") but ultimately inspired by his own dilectum delictum, Crusoe accumulates an impressive list of auxiliary sins on the way to ruin: he becomes disrespectful toward his parents and ultimately rebels against their command, he engages in the standard vices of "loose and unguided" young men, he ignores supernatural warnings, he breaks promises to God. Caught in his own snowballing sinfulness, he loses the "Power" to respond to his "more composed Judgment," like the disobedient children in Bunyan's *Divine Emblems:*

> Their sinful nature prompts them to rebel,
> And to delight in paths that lead to hell.
> Their parents' love and care they overlook,
> As if relation had them quite forsook.
> They take the counsels of the wanton's, rather
> Than the most grave instructions of a father.

And he is even more like the Bible's disobedient children of God.

Crusoe's disobedience closely resembles that of the first man in the Garden and takes its ultimate mythic dimension from the biblical account of the Fall. Two other biblical accounts of disobedience are, however, more in the foreground, for Crusoe discovers that both an Old and a New Testament representative of disobedience are his models. The stories to which Crusoe repeatedly and pointedly alludes, those of Jonah and the prodigal son, were frequently used as exempla by Puritan preachers to warn against restlessness, filial disobedience, and failure to follow one's calling. Typologically, the two stories are similar: they both evince a concern with selfish abdication of one's duty, and they share a pattern of rebellion, flight to a far place, punishment by physical distress, repentance during danger, and a final physical and spiritual deliverance. Crusoe's account follows this general movement, and his life bears even more precise resemblances to the particulars of each story.

The implied moral of the prodigal son parable—that God rejoices over the reclamation of the lost—was less frequently emphasized by Puritan preachers and guide writers than was the more practical literal reading of the first part of the parable. The prodigal son, an emblem of filial disobedience, had fallen by foolish neglect of duty. Technically, he had not disobeyed his father's orders, but his failure to honor his father's position constituted neglect of family duty. Because a father was God's deputy in the family, conduct like that of the prodigal ultimately represented rebellion against God and the divine social order. At a time when the family and other symbols of order appeared to be under severe challenge, the parable seemed dramatically relevant, and guide writers leaned heavily upon its authority. It had the added advantage that the prodigal's return and reward (which were usually interpreted on a "spiritual" level, as well as on the literal level of the story) could argue repentance to those already guilty of rebellion. The parable's effectiveness lay in its forceful illustration of the typical plight of man: alienated from God ("in a far country") by early sin, he constantly faced ever-worsening crises in which he might choose to swallow his pride and return to "his father's house." "A continued Course of Goodness may in it self be more valuable," says Tillotson of the prodigal's actions, "and yet Repentance after a great Fall and long Wandrings may be much more moving and surprizing."

Defoe shapes Crusoe's view of his own state along the lines of the contemporary understanding of the parable. Crusoe first applies the parallel in describing his first voyage, which he had undertaken "without asking God's Blessing, or my Father's, without any Consideration of Circumstances or Consequences." A storm arises, and Crusoe, suddenly aware of the wisdom of his father's advice, resolves that he will "like a true repenting Prodigal, go home to my Father." He makes "many Vows and Resolutions," but when the storm subsides and his "Fears and Apprehensions of being swallow'd up by the Sea [are] forgotten," he abandons these "wise and sober Thoughts." He returns to the rebellious dictates of his "Fancy" and forgets the "Vows and Promises that I made in my Distress": "In . . . one Night's wickedness," he says of his revelry with other sailors, "I drowned all my Repentance, all my Reflections upon my past Conduct, and all my Resolutions for my future." Before the voyage ends, Providence sends a much worse storm (Crusoe decides, in retrospect, that God "resolv'd to leave me entirely without Excuse"), and when his ship capsizes Crusoe has to be rescued by a small boat. "Had I now had the Sense to have gone . . . home," reflects Crusoe later, "I had been happy, and my Father, an Emblem of our Blessed Saviour's Parable, had even Kill'd the fatted Calf for me"; but his "fatal" natural propensity still prevents the proper decision.

Like the prodigal, Crusoe is guilty of the "wicked leaving [of] my Father's House" and of a "Breach of my Duty to God and my Father." Restless and dissatisfied with his lot, he foolishly leaves his family to try his fortunes abroad. Unlike the prodigal, however,

Crusoe refuses to humble himself when brought to distress, and he continues to follow his "Inclination" even though fearful of the results. "I have since often observed," Crusoe reports, "how incongruous and irrational the common Temper of Mankind is, especially of Youth. . . . That they are not asham'd to sin, and yet are asham'd to repent."

In retrospect, Crusoe sees that he should also have learned from Jonah's example, for his life is another redaction of Jonah's story. Like Jonah, Crusoe refuses the calling for which he was divinely appointed, and he defiantly boards a ship to run away. Like Jonah, he finally becomes aware that the storms which plague the ship are sent by God as a punishment for his sin and as a warning to change his course of life. The captain of the ill-fated ship tells Crusoe to interpret his first voyage as *"a plain and visible Token that you are not to be a Seafaring Man."* Perhaps, he suggests, Crusoe was responsible for the ship's disaster, *"like* Jonah *in the Ship of* Tarshish.*"* When he learns Crusoe's life story, he is certain of his interpretation. "What had I done," he asks, "that such an unhappy Wretch should come into my Ship?" The captain's admonition and prophecy (*"where-ever you go, you will meet with nothing but Disasters and Disappointments till your Father's Words are fulfilled upon you"*) causes Crusoe to reflect, and he has "many Struggles with my self, what Course of Life I should take." But until he is brought to despair, like Jonah, in a lonely, apparently hopeless situation, he remains in the rebellious grasp of his natural propensity.

The parable of the prodigal son and the Jonah story both reflect the myth of the Fall (though in a postlapsarian context), and Crusoe's rebellion and punishment parallel the specifics of the account in Genesis even more closely. At the beginning of the novel Crusoe's father portrays Crusoe's station in terms of an Edenic freedom from care— "a Life of Ease and Pleasure." "He told me," says Crusoe, "I might judge of the Happiness of this State, by this one thing, *viz.* That this was the State of Life which all other People envied." It is a station "calculated for all kind of Vertues and all kinds of Enjoyments," characterized by "Peace and Plenty," blessed by "Temperance, Moderation, Quietness, Health, Society, all agreeable Diversions, and all desirable Pleasures." It is designed so that its members may go "silently and smoothly thro' the World, and comfortably out of it, not embarrass'd with the Labours of the Hands or of the Head." This idyllic life is Crusoe's to enjoy without specific obligation; he is required only to accept it contentedly and to eschew the desire of altering his condition. Only the tree of discontent is forbidden: if he tries to leave his station, according to his father's prediction, he will be "the miserablest Wretch that was ever born."

Adam's sin, according to Defoe's contemporaries, stemmed from his restlessness and discontent with his place in Eden. "It was," says Andrew Gray in a sermon on contentment, "*Adams* ignorance of this divine mystery of Christianity, *to be content with every estate, wherein he was placed,* that did bring him down from that high pinacle of his excellency." In effect, Crusoe expels himself from his paradise by committing the forbidden act; like Adam, whose sin had condemned man to a life of wandering in the first place, Crusoe commits the archetypal sin of discontent. Homeless physically and spiritually, he wanders in a world of sin and sickness, storm and shipwreck. Unlike Adam, however, Crusoe does not immediately suffer full punishment: in a post-atonement world where grace prevails, utter desolation and isolation result not from one sin, but from continued rebellion. Only after advice and repeated providential warnings have failed does Crusoe's condition suddenly alter, and instead of the higher station he seeks, he is suddenly reduced "from a Merchant to a miserable Slave." Ironically, his master appoints him to care for his "little Garden," and Crusoe thinks that his situation has reached its nadir. His slavery, however, turns out to be only a "Taste of the Misery I was to go thro," for failure to heed this last warning effects a total archetypal expulsion. On his Bunyanesque *"Island of Despair"* he has to toil by the sweat of his brow, far removed from the paradise with which he had been discontented and even from his "little Garden" parody of it. Ironically, his propensity to roam, to be unconfined, results in complete loss of freedom. Alone in a hostile world, he experiences the isolation of man alienated from his place in the world because he is alienated from his God.

"There are amazing *Judgments* of God," writes Cotton Mather (in explaining that "Evil Pursueth Sinners"), "Where-to Young Men do in *this World* become obnoxious." "And especially," he continues,

> when a notorious *Disobedience to the Voice of their Teachers, and their Parents,* is one Ingredient of their Wickedness. . . .
> There is a *Strange Punishment,* for those *Workers of Iniquity.*
> They become Tragical Examples of Misery and Confusion

under the Judgment of God upon them; Their *Tragedy*
becomes an *History*. They are made Spectacles and Mon-
uments of what the Judgments of God will do upon such
Wretches. The Astonished Spectators cry out, *This is the
Finger of God*. The Just God sets a *Brand* upon them; they
are horribly Mark'd by the *Judgments* of God. They soon
run themselves into horrible Circumstances. The *Tempest*
of God pursues them, and Shipwrecks Them.

Crusoe considers himself a *"Memento"* to others because of the
punishment that befalls him, and he hopes that his life story will
"stand as a Direction from the Experience of the most miserable of
all Conditions in the World." In retrospect, he never doubts that his
difficulties result from his sin. The world, as he views it, is entirely
controlled by God, and, like the providence books, he interprets
both his judgments and his deliverances as "Testimonies . . . of a
secret Hand of Providence governing the World."

Crusoe traces a pattern of warning and punishment in all the
events leading up to his shipwreck. His early ventures result in gradually worsening punishments, but he makes only feeble and brief
gestures toward repentance. On his first voyage, for example, he
encounters two storms, but his religious promptings barely last until
he reaches land. His voyages to Guinea similarly feature warnings—
physical distress, the death of his benefactor, and, finally, his sale
into slavery. Confined in Sallee, he remembers his "Father's
prophetick Discourse" and decides that "now the Hand of Heaven
had overtaken me, and I was undone without Redemption." But
even when he is "deliver'd" and taken to Brazil, he cannot remain
content with the accumulated riches of his new station (a parody of
the paradise he might have enjoyed at home), and he undertakes one
last rebellious voyage.

Crusoe's island imprisonment expands the pattern of punishment. Here, he not only faces physical danger but is effectually pre-
vented from satisfying his major inclination. "Man that will not fear
God willingly," according to Samuel Crossman, "shall be made
(though little to his comfort) to do so by force. That dread of God
which they flee from shall pursue them and overtake them between
the straits."

Crusoe's shipwreck and island isolation derives meaning both
from the theology of the time and from the Puritan metaphor of

man's condition. The sea—still romantic, mysterious, wild, and dangerous to Defoe's contemporaries—was a standard source of punishment for man's wickedness, according to Puritan moralists, who continually point out that the waves can be "the executioners of God's threatening" and that "Winds are sent to fulfill the word of Gods threat." But readers of *Robinson Crusoe* in 1719 would have found Crusoe's sea troubles meaningful for reasons beyond the inherent danger of the sea and its general providential function, for Puritan moralists taught that sin was usually punished in kind. "God chuses," says Timothy Cruso, "oftentimes to *punish* Men in that wherein they most *delight.* He is never more magnified, nor the Sinner more confounded, then when the Sinner's chiefest Joy is turn'd into his *greatest* Sorrow." According to Increase Mather, the appropriateness of punishment to sin may take a variety of forms: God may inflict upon men the same evil that they themselves have committed; the punishments may have *"some Resemblance and Analogy with their Sins"*; the punishments may be brought about by "Instruments" involved in the sin; or sin and punishment may be related "in respect of those Circumstances of Place and Time where and when the Judgment shall take hold of them." Because Crusoe's sin is restlessness and discontent with his place in the divine order, his punishment appropriately removes the possibility of future rebellious wandering. The instrument of his sin (a ship) becomes the instrument of punishment, and the correspondence of time is so striking that Crusoe himself comments upon it. His fatal voyage from Brazil begins on the same day (eight years later) as did his first voyage—September 1. It was, according to Crusoe, "an evil Hour."

More important, Crusoe's isolation epitomizes the Puritan version of the plight of man. Fallen man is alienated from God—separated from him by a wide gulf as a result of sin. He is lonely and isolated in a world for which he was not in the first place intended, but into which he is cast as a result of sin. "Surely," Calvin had said, "no more terrible abyss can be conceived than to feel yourself forsaken and estranged from God; and when you call upon him, not to be heard. It is as if God himself had plotted your ruin." His relationship to God disrupted, Crusoe finds a similar disordering of his relationship to his fellow man and to his environment. His punishment, like other significant developments in *Robinson Crusoe,* converts a fundamental religious metaphor into the specifics of experience, achieving a peculiar unity of physical and spiritual levels—a unity enforced and exploited much further as the downward cycle ends and Crusoe learns that "deliverance" has more than one meaning, and that to be alone may also mean to be "singled out."

Crusoe, says Irving Howe, "never indulges in introspection. I do not think there is one statement of self-analysis in the book." Such a view reflects a rather blind commitment to the premises of "modern" psychology and represents a refusal to consider *Robinson Crusoe* in its own historical setting or on its own terms. Crusoe does not, of course, attempt to peer into his psyche or pull back the curtains of his subconscious. Unlike modern psychological novels, which find ultimate answers within the limits of one man's mind, *Robinson Crusoe* depends upon the broader conception of God's providential control, within which the individual human drama must be played. Man can only seek to apprehend causes which are beyond his control and to which he must acclimate himself. *Robinson Crusoe*'s philosophy and psychology look backward rather than forward, but, in the book's own historical terms, Crusoe's search for understanding is both introspective and self-analytical. In fact, the narrative point of view and the ultimate structure of the novel depend upon Crusoe's introspective framework. All of the novel's events are recounted by a narrator who has had more than thirty years to reflect on the "meanings" of such actions as a flight from home or such states as slavery, shipwreck, and solitude.

The subtleties of the retrospective first-person narration are easy to overlook, for the sequence seems natural and artless. Event follows event in roughly chronological order, and the more important episodes are presented scenically, to use Lubbock's distinction, with elaborate descriptions of setting and liberal use of dialogue and monologue. Defoe also employs such devices of immediacy as a "journal" (presumably written daily, to record events at the time when they occurred) and the stockpiling of small details (which, by emphasizing the amount of recall, tend to blur the time factor). A later perspective on these events is, however, implicit in the selectivity employed, and often this perspective is explicit in the account. Even the "journal" section is infused with later interpretation. Crusoe does not simply transcribe his daily jottings (contrary to his promise that "I shall here give you the Copy"), but "edits" them freely from a later perspective. His first journal entry is September 30, 1659, but after two days of entries (less than one page of text, which might well be "copied" from an original "journal"), Crusoe begins to contract and expand the account. The next twenty-four days of the journal are collapsed into two sentences; a few pages later Crusoe interrupts the journal account for three months, substituting a general account of progress and a description of scattered, fleeting religious promptings which he felt during that time. This description is clearly retrospective: in it he mentions events which occur three years later. Many subsequent entries could be copied from a journal, but in some places a later point of view is superimposed, without previous warning. Even in sections calculated to produce the illusion of present action, Defoe uses the double time scheme to suggest movement and direction in Crusoe's life pattern and, ultimately, to suggest the structure of the novel itself.

We must recognize how the retrospective point of view works in *Robinson Crusoe* to understand the schematization of Crusoe's life, for the deceptively simple chronological record is infused throughout with later interpretation. Critics have often complained of Crusoe's moral monologues, finding them tedious and superfluous, but they have not often recognized that these reflections reinforce meanings implicit in the recounting of events. Crusoe's view of life is a unified conception, arrived at after a lifetime of thought and evaluation, and evident both in his after-the-fact account of episodes and in his elaborate interpretive monologues. (Starr's treatment of *Robinson Crusoe*'s relation to spiritual autobiography does not, I think, take adequate account of Defoe's use of this double time scheme. Personal diaries usually record events soon after they happen [the immediacy of which Richardson tries to capture in his "writing to the moment" device]; ordinarily, a more cohesive and pointed retrospective treatment of a saint's pattern of life results only from a decision to present the life publicly. The aim of diaries is always to *discover* the pattern, but Defoe employs his time scheme to *articulate* the pattern early in his narrative. Richardson's technique of allowing the life pattern to manifest itself gradually is much closer to the methods of journals and spiritual autobiographies.) Throughout the narrative he alludes to the pattern of his life, a pattern set up by his early disobedience and flight. Retrospectively, he notes the causal sequence of events: punishment inevitably follows disobedience; failure to heed repeated warnings intensifies both the seriousness of the sin and its practical results. Like the Puritan biographers, Crusoe seeks to determine the original cause of his physical and spiritual plight, and from this cause he traces all the events in the downward cycle. But, like the heroes of spiritual biography, Crusoe is saved physically and spiritually by the specific intervention of God, and from this intervention he traces the upward cycle. Looking back upon the history of his life, he can see the purposeful pattern of events; he is able to decipher "Providence's Checquer-Work."

Retrospection is not necessarily introspection, of course; one may look back without evaluation of causes, without assessment of one's own responsibility for involvement. But Crusoe is introspective just as Puritan diarists are introspective: he searches the events of his life for threads of meaning and examines his own acts of will in terms of a philosophy revealed to him after he had surrendered himself to a purposeful universe. What he finds is not just an occasional thread but a personal fabric of meaning, which is part of the carefully woven divine quilt of history. Far from lacking introspection, Crusoe, from the time of his conversion, reflects almost constantly upon his choices and their meanings, and he relates all of his strange and surprising adventures to a pattern that his reflections reveal to him.

Crusoe's retrospection and introspection produce a good deal of personal discomfort, for the more he thinks about his past, the more he blames himself for the difficulties he encounters. When he begins to see his own responsibility, however, he begins to understand the cause-effect process in his world and develops a desire to harmonize himself with the First Cause so that he can exchange "Misery" for "Happiness." The big step in his harmonizing process is his repentance and conversion. This step comes about when his desires have been fully prepared, and it involves direct supernatural intervention in his life. Once his desire is whetted and once that intervention comes, Crusoe's life can never again be the same, nor can his view of that life. For as divine illumination dramatically touches him, as revelation is added to his discursive powers, retrospection and introspection become literally one—and the pattern of his life becomes not only changed but understood in cosmic terms.

Myth and Fiction in *Robinson Crusoe*

Leopold Damrosch, Jr.

MIMESIS, ALLEGORY, AND THE AUTONOMOUS SELF

In 1719, at the age of fifty-nine, the businessman, pamphleteer, and sometime secret agent Daniel Defoe unexpectedly wrote the first English novel. The affinities of *Robinson Crusoe* with the Puritan tradition are unmistakable: it draws on the genres of spiritual autobiography and allegory, and Crusoe's religious conversion is presented as the central event. But this primal novel, in the end, stands as a remarkable instance of a work that gets away from its author, and gives expression to attitudes that seem to lie far from his conscious intention. Defoe sets out to dramatize the conversion of the Puritan self, and he ends by celebrating a solitude that exalts autonomy instead of submission. He undertakes to show the dividedness of a sinner, and ends by projecting a hero so massively self-enclosed that almost nothing of his inner life is revealed. He proposes a naturalistic account of real life in a real world, and ends by creating an immortal triumph of wish-fulfillment. To some extent, of course, Defoe must have been aware of these ambiguities, which are summed up when Crusoe calls the island "my reign, or my captivity, which you please." But it is unlikely that he saw how deep the gulf was that divided the two poles of his story, the Augustinian theme of alienation and the romance theme of gratification.

Recommending *Robinson Crusoe* to his readers as a didactic work, Defoe compared it to *The Pilgrim's Progress* and called it "an allusive

From *God's Plot and Man's Stories*. ©1985 by the University of Chicago. University of Chicago Press, 1985.

allegoric history" designed to promote moral ends, in terms which explicitly distinguish this kind of writing from immortal fictions that are no better than lies:

> The selling [sic] or writing a parable, or an allusive allegoric history, is quite a different case [from lying], and is always distinguished from this other jesting with truth, that it is designed and effectually turned for instructive and upright ends, and has its moral justly applied. Such are the historical parables in the Holy Scriptures, such "The Pilgrim's Progress," and such, in a word, the adventures of your fugitive friend, "Robinson Crusoe."

Crusoe's "original sin," like Adam's, is disobedience to his father. After going to sea against express warnings, he is punished by shipwreck and isolation, converted by God (who communicates through a monitory dream during sickness, an earthquake, and the words of the Bible), and rewarded in the end beyond his fondest hopes. More than once Crusoe likens himself to the prodigal son, a favorite emblem for fallen man in Puritan homiletics, and a shipwrecked sea captain indignantly calls him a Jonah. In the providential scheme his sojourn on the island is both punishment and deliverance: punishment, because his wandering disposition must be rebuked; deliverance, because he (alone of the crew) is saved from drowning and then converted by grace that overcomes the earlier "hardening" of his heart. As Ben Gunn summarizes a similar lesson in *Treasure Island,* "It were Providence that put me here. I've thought it all out in this here lonely island, and I'm back on piety."

Yet Defoe's story curiously fails to sustain the motif of the prodigal. His father is long dead when Crusoe finally returns—there is no tearful reunion, no fatted calf, not even a sad visit to the father's grave—and by then he has come into a fortune so splendid that he exclaims, "I might well say, now indeed, that the latter end of Job was better than the beginning." Far from punishing the prodigal Crusoe for disobedience, the novel seems to reward him for enduring a mysterious test. Crusoe's father had wanted him to stay at home and, two elder sons having vanished without a trace, to establish his lineage in a strange land (he was "a foreigner of Bremen" named Kreutznaer). But "a secret over-ruling decree" pushes Crusoe on toward his wayfaring fate, and it is hard not to feel that he does well to submit to it, like the third son in the fairy tales whom magical success awaits.

Robinson Crusoe is the first of a series of novels by Defoe that present the first-person reminiscences of social outsiders, adventurers and criminals. Since the Puritans were nothing if not outsiders, the "masterless men" of the seventeenth century can appear (as Walzer observes) either as religious pilgrims or as picaresque wayfarers. Whether as saints or as rogues they illustrate the equivocal status of the individual who no longer perceives himself fixed in society. And by Defoe's time the attempt to create a counter-*nomos* in the Puritan small group—Bunyan's separated church—was increasingly a thing of the past. Puritanism was subsiding into bourgeois Nonconformity, no longer an ideology committed to reshaping the world, but rather a social class seeking religious "toleration" and economic advantage. The old Puritans, glorying in their differentness, would have regarded the Nonconformists as all too eager to conform.

Defoe was both beneficiary and victim of the new ethic, and two facts are particularly relevant to the allegorical implications of *Crusoe:* he was twice disastrously bankrupt during a rocky career as capitalist and speculator, and he regretted an unexplained failure to enter the Presbyterian ministry—"It was my disaster," he says mysteriously in his one reference to the subject, "first to be set apart for, and then to be set apart from, the honour of that sacred employ." John Richetti, in the subtlest interpretation of *Crusoe* that we have, sees Defoe as celebrating a mastery of self and environment which implicitly contradicts his religious premises: "The narrative problem . . . is to allow Crusoe to achieve and enjoy freedom and power without violating the restrictions of a moral and religious ideology which defines the individual as less than autonomous." But the tension was always present in the ideology itself; it grows directly from the implications of a faith like Bunyan's, in which temptations are projected outside the self and determinism is a force with which one learns to cooperate. What is new is the effective withdrawal of God from a structure which survives without him, though its inhabitants continue in all sincerity to pay him homage.

At the level of conscious intention Defoe undoubtedly wanted *Robinson Crusoe* to convey a conventional doctrinal message. The island probably suggests the debtors' prison in which he was humiliatingly confined, and it certainly allegorizes the solitude of soul needed for repentance and conversion. "I was a prisoner," Crusoe exclaims, "locked up with the eternal bars and bolts of the ocean. . . . This would break out upon me like a storm, and make me wring my hands and weep like a child." Very much in the Puritan tradition Crusoe learns to recognize the "particular providences" with which God controls his life. When he discovers turtles on the other side of the island he thinks himself unlucky to have come ashore on the barren side, and only afterwards realizes, on finding the ghastly remains of a cannibal feast, "that it was a special providence that I was cast upon the side of the island where the savages never came." Once aware of the cannibals he must find a cave in which to conceal his fire, and Providence, having permitted him years of conspicuous fires without harm, now provides the very thing he needs. "The mouth of this hollow was at the bottom of a great rock, where by mere accident (I would say, if I did not see abundant reason to ascribe all such things now to providence) I was cutting down some thick branches of trees to make charcoal. Most notably of all, Crusoe is rescued from hunger when some spilled chicken-feed sprouts apparently by chance; eventually he understands that although it was natural for the seeds to grow, it was miraculous that they did so in a way that was advantageous to him.

In a Puritan view the normal course of nature is simply the sum total of an ongoing chain of special providences, for as a modern expositor of Calvin puts it, "Bread is not the natural product of the earth. In order that the earth may provide the wheat from which it is made, God must intervene, ceaselessly and ever anew, in the 'order of nature,' must send the rain and dew, must cause the sun to rise every morning." In the eighteenth century, however, there was an increasing tendency to define providence as the general order of things rather than as a series of specific interventions. Wesley bitterly remarked that "The doctrine of a particular providence is absolutely out of fashion in England—and any but a particular providence is no providence at all." One purpose of *Robinson Crusoe* is to vindicate God's omnipotence by showing the folly of making such a distinction. And Crusoe's isolation (like Ben Gunn's) encourages him to think the matter through. When Moll Flanders, in Defoe's next major novel, is finally arrested and thrown into Newgate, she suddenly perceives her clever career as the condign punishment of "an inevitable and unseen fate." But she admits that she is a poor moralist and unable to retain the lesson for long: "I had no sense of my condition, no thought of heaven or hell at least, that went any farther than a bare flying touch, like the stitch or pain that gives a hint and goes off." Moll sees only at moments of crisis what Crusoe learns to see consistently.

In keeping with this message the narrative contains many scriptural allusions, which are often left tacit for the reader to detect and ponder. The sprouting wheat, for instance, recalls a central doctrine of the Gospels: "Verily, verily I say unto you, Except a corn of wheat fall into the ground and die, it abideth alone; but if it die, it bringeth forth much fruit. He that loveth his life shall lose it, and he that hateth his life in this world shall keep it unto life eternal" (John 12:24–25). Crusoe's life recapitulates that of everyman, a fictional equivalent of what Samuel Clarke recommended in the study of history: "By setting before us what hath been, it premonisheth us of what will be again; sith the self-same fable is acted over again in the world, the persons only are changed that act it." Like other Puritans Crusoe has to grope toward the meaning of the types embodied in his own biography. Defoe often likened himself to persecuted figures in the Bible, but wrote to his political master Harley that his life "has been and yet remains a mystery of providence unexpounded." Translating his experience into the quasi-allegory of *Crusoe* permits him to define typological connections more confidently, from the coincidence of calendar dates to the overarching theme of deliverance (typified in individuals like Jonah, and in the children of Israel released from Egypt). Thus the temporal world, however circumstantially described, can be seen in the Puritan manner as gathered up into eternity. Crusoe's fever is not only a direct warning from God but also, as Alkon shows, a rupture in his careful recording of chronology by which he is "wrenched outside time," an intimation that the various incidents in the story must be subsumed in a single structure. As in other Puritan narratives, separate moments are valued for their significance in revealing God's will, and become elements in an emblematic pattern rather than constituents of a causal sequence.

Nearly all of the essential issues cluster around the crucial theme of solitude. Defoe clearly gives it a positive valuation, and suggests more than once that Crusoe could have lived happily by himself forever if no other human beings had intruded. "I was now in my twenty-third year of residence in this island, and was so naturalized to the place, and to the manner of living, that could I have but enjoyed the certainty that no savages would come to the place to disturb me, I could have been content to have capitulated for spending the rest of my time there, even to the last moment, till I had laid me down and died like the old goat in the cave." However obliquely Defoe's *Serious Reflections of Robinson Crusoe* (published in the following year) relates to the novel, it must be significant that it begins with an essay "Of Solitude" which moves at once to the claim that we are solitary even in the midst of society:

> Everything revolves in our minds by innumerable circular motions, all centering in ourselves. . . . All reflection is carried home, and our dear self is, in one respect, the end of living. Hence man may be properly said to be alone in the midst of the crowds and hurry of men and business. . . . Our meditations are all solitude in perfection; our passions are all exercised in retirement; we love, we hate, we covet, we enjoy, all in privacy and solitude. All that we communicate of those things to any other is but for their assistance in the pursuit of our desires; the end is at home; the enjoyment, the contemplation, is all solitude and retirement; it is for ourselves we enjoy, and for ourselves we suffer.

Critics have unfairly quoted this disturbing and memorable passage as symptomatic of a peculiar egotism in Defoe. In fact it reflects the logical consequence of Puritan inwardness, also susceptible of course to the charge of egotism—the descent into the interior self that impels Bunyan's Christian to reject his family in order to win eternal life. And it is compatible, as Defoe goes on to make clear, with the traditional view that "Man is a creature so formed for society, that it may not only be said that it is not good for him to be alone, but 'tis really impossible he should be alone." The good man or woman ought to associate with others but seek in meditation that solitude which can be attained anywhere, symbolized in *Robinson Crusoe* by "the life of a man in an island."

In effect Defoe literalizes the metaphor that Descartes (for example) uses: "Among the crowds of a large and active people . . . I have been able to live as solitary and retired as in the remotest desert." But to literalize the metaphor creates profound complications, for it is one thing to live *as if* on a desert island and another to do it in earnest. Jonathan Edwards writes that in his meditations on the Song of Songs, "an inward sweetness . . . would carry me away in my contemplations, . . . and sometimes a kind of vision, or fixed ideas and imaginations, of being alone in the mountains, or some solitary wilderness, far from all mankind, sweetly conversing with Christ, and wrapt and swallowed up in God." This rapture of self-abnegation is very far from Crusoe's experience. The difference is partly explained by the bluff common sense of Crusoe, not to mention of Defoe; Dickens comments, "I have no doubt he was a precious dry disagreeable article himself." But beyond that it is due to the way in which Defoe takes a topos of allegory and literalizes it in mimetic narrative. Even though he may believe that the result is still allegorical, he has tranformed—to borrow a useful pair of terms from German—*Jenseitigkeit* into *Diesseitigkeit,* collapsing the "other side" of religion into the "this side" of familiar experience. In *The Pilgrim's Progress* everyday images serve as visualizable emblems of an interior experience that belongs to another world. In *Robinson Crusoe* there is no other world.

Another way of saying this is that *Crusoe* reflects the progressive desacralizing of the world that was implicit in Protestantism, and that ended (in Weber's phrase) by disenchanting it altogether. Defoe's God may work through nature, but he does so by "natural" cause and effect (the seeds that sprout), and nature itself is not viewed as sacramental. Rather it is the workplace where man is expected to labor until it is time to go to a heaven too remote and hypothetical to ask questions about. "I come from the City of Destruction," Bunyan's Christian says, "but am going to Mount Sion." In *Crusoe,* as is confirmed by the feeble sequel *The Farther Adventures of Robinson Crusoe,* there is no goal at all, at least not in this world. But the world of *The Pilgrim's Progress* was *not* this world: after conversion the believer knew himself to be a stranger in a strange land. Defoe keeps the shape of the allegorical scheme but radically revalues its content.

Defoe is no metaphysician, and his dislocation of the religious schema may seem naive, but in practice if not in theory it subtly images the ambiguity of man's relation to his world, at once a "natural" home and a resistant object to be manipulated. Milton's Adam and Eve fall from the world in which they had been at home, and Bunyan's characters march through the fallen world like soldiers passing through enemy territory. Defoe has it both ways, defining man over against nature and at the same time inventing a fantasy of perfect union with it. As technologist and (halting) thinker Crusoe finds himself in opposition to nature, as when he builds a "periagua" so grotesquely huge that he is unable to drag it to the water, or when he does make a successful canoe but is nearly swept out to sea by unexpected currents. And his concepts function to define his human status in contrast with nature, in keeping with the moral tradition that saw man in a "state of nature" as living in continual fear of death. But as a concord fiction *Robinson Crusoe* still more strongly suggests that man can indeed return to union with nature, so long as other men are not present to disturb him. In important respects the island is an Eden.

This equivocation between punitive doctrine and liberating romance has remarkable consequences in Defoe's treatment of psychology. In effect he carries to its logical conclusion the externalizing of unwanted impulses which we have seen in Bunyan and other Puritan writers. With God generalized into an abstract Providence, Crusoe's universe is peopled by inferior beings, angelic spirits who guide him with mysterious hints and diabolical spirits who seek his ruin. Of these the latter are the more interesting, and Crusoe is scandalized to find that Friday is unaware of any Satan, merely saying "O" to a pleasant but ineffectual deity called Benamuckee who seems not to know how to punish men. Defoe needs the Devil—and this must be his never-articulated answer to Friday's trenchant question, "Why God no kill the Devil?"—because man's unacknowledged impulses have to be explained. Like the older Puritans Defoe externalizes such impulses by calling them tricks of Satan, but he altogether lacks the subtle dialectic by which the Puritans acknowledged man's continued complicity with the hated enslaver.

Defoe's late work *The Political History of the Devil* (1726), once one gets behind its frequent facetiousness, expresses deep anxiety about the power of a being who "is with us, and sometimes in us, sees when he is not seen, hears when he is not heard, comes in without leave, and goes out without noise; is neither to be shut in or shut out." Yet in a sense this ominous figure is welcome, for he furnishes a comforting explanation of feelings which must otherwise be located in one's self. After discussing the case of virtuous persons whom the Devil causes to behave lasciviously in their dreams, Defoe tells the haunting story of a tradesman, "in great distress for money in his business," who dreamt that he was walking "all alone in a great wood" where he met a little child with a bag of gold and a diamond necklace, and was prompted by the Devil to rob and kill the child.

He need do no more but twist the neck of it a little, or crush it with his knee; he told me he stood debating with himself, whether he should do so or not; but that in that instant his heart struck him with the word Murther, and he entertained an horror of it, refused to do it, and immediately waked. He told me that when he waked he found himself in so violent a sweat as he had never known the like; that his pulse beat with that heat and rage, that it was like a palpitation of the heart to him; and that the agitation of his spirits was such that he was not fully composed in some hours; though the satisfaction and joy that attended him, when he found it was but a dream, assisted much to return his spirits to their due temperament.

One may well suspect that this desperate and guilty tradesman was Defoe himself, and perhaps it is not fanciful to think that the famous episode in *Moll Flanders,* in which Moll robs a child of its watch but resists the temptation to kill it, is a kind of revision and expiation of the dream. Guilty impulses like these are doubly repudiated on Crusoe's island: first, because they are projected on to Satan and the cannibals whom Satan prompts, and second, because so long as Crusoe is alone he could not act upon them even if he wanted to. The return of human beings means the return of the possibility of sin, as indeed he realizes when he longs to gun down the cannibals in cold blood.

In *Robinson Crusoe,* therefore, we see the idea of solitude undergoing a drastic revaluation. Instead of representing a descent into the self for the purpose of repentance, it becomes the normal condition of all selves as they confront the world in which they have to survive. Puritans of Bunyan's generation sometimes welcomed imprisonment because it freed them from external pressures and made self-scrutiny easier. Baxter for example says, "If you be banished, imprisoned, or left alone, it is but a relaxation from your greatest labours; which though you may not cast off yourselves, you may lawfully be sensible of your ease, if God take off your burden. It is but a cessation from your sharpest conflicts, and removal from a multitude of great temptations." This liberation from outer attacks, however, was supposed to encourage a deeper attention to inner conflict, as in the widespread custom of keeping diaries. But that is precisely what Crusoe does not do. He keeps his diary *before* conversion, and stops with the flimsy excuse (on the part of the novelist) that he ran out of ink and could not figure out how to make any. At the very moment when the Puritan's continuous self-analysis begins, Crusoe's ends.

The function of Crusoe's diary, it seems, is not to anatomize the self, but rather to keep track of it in the modern fashion that Riesman describes: "The diary-keeping that is so significant a symptom of the new type of character may be viewed as a kind of inner time-and-motion study by which the individual records and judges his output day by day. It is evidence of the separation between the behaving and the scrutinizing self." This new way of presenting psychology goes far toward explaining what critics of every persuasion have recognized, the peculiar opacity and passivity of character in Defoe's fiction. Novak observes that "frequently a passion appears to be grafted on to the characters, an appendage rather than an organic part of them," and Price says that "conflicts are settled in Crusoe or for him, not by him." And it also helps to explain why, as Fletcher notices in his survey of allegory, much in Crusoe is dispersed into externalized daemonic agents. A similar procedure made Bunyan's Christian seem more complex and human by analyzing his psyche into complex elements; it makes Crusoe seem, if not less human, at least less intelligible, because we are encouraged to look outward rather than inward. So long as we imagine ourselves looking outward *with* Crusoe, we see what he sees and feel what he feels, but what we perceive is always external. Starr shows in a brilliant essay that Defoe's prose constantly projects feelings on to the outer world, and that the reality thus presented is subjective rather than interior, a defense of the ego "by animating, humanizing, and Anglicizing the alien thing he encounters." If we try to look *into* any of Defoe's characters we find ourselves baffled; when Crusoe, on seeing the footprint, speaks of being "confused and out of my self," we have no clear idea of what kind of self he has when he is in it.

In Defoe's behaviorist psychology, as in that of Hobbes, people live by reacting to external stimuli, and while we may get a strong sense of individuality, there is little sense of the psyche. His frightened behavior after seeing the footprint, Crusoe says, "would have made any one have thought I was haunted with an evil conscience." If beasts and savages are allegorical symbols of inner impulses, then of course he does have an evil conscience; but in the mimetic fiction they are simply beasts and savages, and conscience becomes irrelevant. Moreover Crusoe describes how he *would have looked* to an people was precisely what made him comfortable, and the advent of other people is what filled him with horrible fears. Riesman's point about the split between the behaving and the observing self is thus confirmed.

In contrast with the self the Puritans believed in, utterly open to God and potentially open to careful introspection, the self in Defoe participates in the general cultural revaluation epitomized by Locke: "Man, though he has great variety of thoughts, and such from which others as well as himself might receive profit and delight; yet they are all within his own breast, invisible and hidden from others, nor can of themselves be made to appear." Locke goes on to describe the role of language in bridging (but not abolishing) this gap by means of conventional signs. Hume characteristically goes further and argues that the self is invisible *to itself* as well as to others: "Ourself, independent of the perception of every other object, is in reality nothing; for which reason we must turn our view to external objects." This psychology is quite directly a rejection of Puritan introspection, which is not surprising since Locke championed toleration against fanaticism—he wrote a book entitled *The Reasonableness of Christianity*—and Hume turned atheist after a Calvinist upbringing. If God can see every hidden corner of the self, the believer is obliged to try to see it too; but if God withdraws or vanishes, then the anguish of self-examination is no longer necessary.

These considerations suggest a way of reconciling two very different interpretations of Crusoe's psychology. One holds that the self is fragmented in a state of turbulent flux, the other that the self precedes and resists alteration: "We always feel as we read that personality is radically primary, that it existed before events and continues to exist in spite of circumstances that seek to change or even to obliterate it." In effect this is the distinction, already noted, between solitude as self-abnegating introspection and solitude as self-assertive independence. Whenever Defoe allows his narrators to try to look within, they do indeed find a chaos of unfocused sensations, but most of the time they simply avoid introspection and assert themselves tenaciously against a series of manageable challenges. The notoriously extraneous ending of *Robinson Crusoe*, in which the hero successfully organizes his traveling party to fight off wolves in the Pyrenees, may symbolize the mastery that Crusoe has attained on the island, but if so it is a mastery of external objects rather than a richer organization of the psyche. No wonder all of Defoe's characters, like their creator, habitually resort to alias and disguise.

This assertion of the autonomy of the self is mirrored in the disappearance of Crusoe's father, with his oracular warning, "That boy might be happy if he would stay at home, but if he goes abroad he will be the miserablest wretch that was ever born." What the miserable wretch gets is an idyllic, self-sufficient existence that for generations has made *Robinson Crusoe* a special favorite of children. And Crusoe thereby achieves what Milton's Satan so heretically desired, a condition of self-creation. Despite its mimetic surface, *Robinson Crusoe* closely anticipates the Romantic pattern discussed by Bloom: "All quest-romances of the post-Enlightenment, meaning all Romanticisms whatsoever, are quests to re-beget one's own self, to become one's own Great Original."

The Romantic poets and philosophers interpreted the Fall as the birth of consiousness of one's finite self, and Blake explicitly identified it with the onset of puberty. *Robinson Crusoe* is a resolutely sexless novel, with only the most covert prurience: "I could not perceive by my nicest observation but that they were stark naked, and had not the least covering upon them; but whether they were men or women, that I could not distinguish." In fact, *Crusoe* is a fantasy of retreat into an innocence before puberty, with a vision of solitude among vegetable riches that literalizes the metaphors of Marvell's "Garden":

> Such was that happy garden-state,
> While man there walked without a mate:
> After a place so pure and sweet,
> What other help could yet be meet!
> But 'twas beyond a mortal's share
> To wander solitary there:
> Two paradises 'twere in one
> To live in paradise alone.

Milton's sober Puritanism leads him to elaborate the ways in which the original helpmeets drag each other down, while implying the unacceptability of Marvell's playful fantasy of life without a mate. But Marvell was after all a Puritan, and wrote somberly elsewhere that every man must be "his own expositor, his own both minister and people, bishop and diocese, his own council; and his conscience excusing or condemning him, accordingly he escapes or incurs his own internal anathema." Defoe evades the internal anathema, invents a world without sexuality, and gives a positive valuation to the shelter behind a wall of trees which in *Paradise Lost* was a guilty escape from God's eye:

> O might I here
> In solitude live savage, in some glade
> Obscured, where highest woods impenetrable
> To star or sunlight, spread their umbrage broad.
>
> (9.1084–87)

Adam and Eve are expelled from Eden and sent out into the world of history; Crusoe retreats from history into an Eden innocent of sexuality and of guilt. To be sure, Defoe makes him now and then refer to his "load of guilt" or bewail "the wicked, cursed, abominable life I led all the past part of my days," but no details are ever given, and on the island the absence of other people makes guilt irrelevant.

Solitude is power. "There were no rivals. I had no competitor, none to dispute sovereignty or command with me." And again: "It would have made a Stoic smile to have seen me and my little family sit down to dinner; there was my majesty the prince and lord of the whole island; I had the lives of all my subjects at my absolute command. I could hang, draw, give liberty, and take it away, and no rebels among all my subjects." The subjects are a parrot, a dog, and two cats; the cruelties that might tempt a despot among men would be absurd among pets. Christianity always dealt uneasily with Stoicism, which recommended an indifference to the world that seemed appealing, but also a preoccupation with self that seemed un-Christian. Regal in solitude, Crusoe would indeed make a Stoic smile. Absolute power is a function of freedom from social power; only when the cannibals arrive does the Hobbesian state of nature resume, as Defoe describes it in his poem *Jure Divino* (1706):

> Nature has left this tincture in the blood,
> That all men would be tyrants if they could.
> If they forbear their neighbours to devour,
> 'Tis not for want of will, but want of power.

So long as he is by himself Crusoe escapes Hobbes's war of all against all and rejoices in the war of nobody against nobody.

Defoe makes it absolutely explicit that Crusoe's Eden is an escape from guilt. "I was removed from all the wickedness of the world here. I had neither the *lust of the flesh, the lust of the eye, or the pride of life*" (the reference is to a favorite Puritan text, John 2:16). To be alone with God is to be alone with oneself and to find it good:

> Thus I lived mighty comfortably, my mind being entirely composed of resigning to the will of God, and throwing myself wholly upon the disposal of his Providence. This made my life better than sociable, for when I began to regret the want of conversation, I would ask my self whether thus conversing mutually with my own thoughts, and, as I hope I may say, with even God himself by ejaculations, was not better than the utmost enjoyment of human society in the world.

Crusoe has nothing to hide. Whereas Bunyan trembled in the knowledge that God sees "the most secret thoughts of the heart," Crusoe often applies the word "secret" to emotions of self-satisfaction: "I descended a little on the side of that delicious vale, surveying it with a secret kind of pleasure." This is not the Puritan use of the term, but an ethical and aesthetic ideal that Defoe may have picked up from Addison: "A man of a polite imagination . . . meets with a secret refreshment in a description, and often feels a greater satisfaction in the prospect of fields and meadows than another does in the possession." The solitary Crusoe has no one to keep secrets from; the word "secret" defines his privacy, individuality, possessiveness, and sole claim to pleasure.

Self-congratulation merges with the frequently mentioned "secret hints" of Providence until Crusoe learns to identify Providence with his own desires. When after a time he reflects on his role in saving Friday from paganism, "A secret joy run through every part of my soul." For the older Puritans determinism was a crucial issue, whether one concluded like Milton that man was free to cooperate with God's will in his own way, or like Bunyan that man must learn to make his will conform to the irresistible force of predestination. In strictly theological terms Defoe seems to have followed Baxter in stressing God's desire to welcome all of his children, rather than his power of predestination. But imaginatively Defoe shares with the Puritans a feeling of unfreedom, of being compelled to act by some power beyond himself. In the imaginary world of fiction he can embrace that power instead of resisting it. In its simplest terms this amounts to asserting that Crusoe is an agent of Providence as well as its beneficiary, as he himself indicates after masterminding the defeat of the mutineers:

> "Gentlemen," said I, "do not be surprised at me; perhaps you may have a friend near you when you did not expect it." "He must be sent directly from heaven, then," said one of them very gravely to me, and pulling off his hat at the same time to me, "for our condition is past the help of man." "All help is from heaven, sir," said I.

But beyond this, Defoe's determinism becomes a defense of his own impulses, whereas for Puritans it would have been a confirmation of their sinfulness. Providence is seen as responsible not only for what happens but also for what does not, for what Crusoe is not as well as what he is. "Had Providence . . . blessed me with confined desires" none of the misfortunes—and none of the rewards—would have come about. But Providence did not. Where then does responsibility lie?

The more one ponders this question, the more equivocal the role of Providence becomes, as is vividly apparent when Crusoe reflects on his very first shipwreck.

> Had I now had the sense to have gone back to Hull and have gone home, I had been happy, and my father, an emblem of our blessed Saviour's parable, had even killed the fatted calf for me; for hearing the ship I went away in was cast away in Yarmouth Road, it was a great while before he had any assurance that I was not drowned.
>
> But my ill fate pushed me on now with an obstinacy that nothing could resist; and though I had several times loud calls from my reason and my more composed judgment to go home, yet I had no power to do it. I know not what to call this, nor will I urge that it is a secret overruling decree that hurries us on to be the instruments of our own destruction, even though it be before us, and that we rush upon with our eyes open. Certainly nothing but some such decreed unavoidable misery attending, and which it was impossible for me to escape, could have pushed me forward against the calm reasonings and persuasions of my

most retired thoughts, and against two such visible in-
structions as I had met with in my first attempt.

The passage is filled with interesting negatives: (1) Crusoe would
have been like the prodigal if he had gone home, but he did *not;* (2)
he will *not* say that his fate was compelled by "a secret overruling
decree"; (3) yet *nothing but* such a decree can account for it.

One can try to explain these complications in orthodox Christian fashion, as Coleridge does:

> When once the mind, in despite of the remonstrating con-
> science, has abandoned its free power to a haunting im-
> pulse or idea, than whatever tends to give depth and
> vividness to this idea or indefinite imagination increases its
> despotism, and in the same proportion renders the reason
> and free will ineffectual. . . . This is the moral of
> Shakespeare's *Macbeth,* and the true solution of this para-
> graph—not any overruling decree of divine wrath, but the
> tyranny of the sinner's own evil imagination, which he has
> voluntarily chosen as his master.

Coleridge adds, "Rebelling against his conscience he becomes the
slave of his own furious will." But Crusoe does not go so far as this
toward accepting the orthodox solution. He shows that he is aware
of it, and hence hesitates to ascribe misfortunes to fate or God, but
nevertheless the sense of involuntary behavior is so strong that he can
only attribute it to "some such decreed unavoidable misery."

An emphasis on God's "decrees," comforting for the elect and
dreadful for the reprobate, was fundamental to Calvinism. But
Crusoe uses Calvinist language here to suggest that he cannot be
morally responsible for actions in which he is moved about like a
chess piece. In many places Defoe discusses the kinds of necessity in
ordinary life (finding food, self-defense) that may not extenuate crime
but impel it so irresistibly that the criminal is simply not free to
behave otherwise. A character in *Colonel Jack* says, "I believe my case
was what I find is the case of most of the wicked part of the world,
viz. that to be reduced to necessity is to be wicked; for necessity is
not only the temptation, but is such a temptation as human nature is
not empowered to resist. How good then is that God which takes
from you, sir, the temptation, by taking away the necessity?" Surely

the corollary must also hold: the sinner can hardly be blamed if God does *not* remove the temptation by removing the necessity.

Obeying necessity, Crusoe allows himself to ride the current of his secret destiny and is magnificently rewarded. A Puritan reading of *Robinson Crusoe*—such as Defoe himself might have endorsed—would hold that by seeking self-fulfillment and creating a private *nomos,* Crusoe is an abject sinner. But the logic of the story denies this. Starr has shown that Defoe was fascinated with the science of casuistry, which treats necessity as an ethical excuse for behavior instead of—as in Calvinism—a moral condemnation of it. The inverted egotism of Bunyan's "chief of sinners" is turned right-side-up again, as Crusoe's island refuses to remain a metaphor for captivity and quickly develops positive qualities. Since Crusoe is a fictional character and not a real person, what is really involved is Defoe's imaginative conception of the island. And this at bottom is a powerful fantasy of punishment that can be willingly accepted because it ceases to punish. The autonomy of solitude is the happy culmination of those mysterious impulses that first sent Crusoe to sea, and in achieving it he makes his destiny his choice.

The much-discussed economic aspects of *Robinson Crusoe* are suggestive of ambiguities very like the religious ones. On this topic the locus classicus is Ian Watt's chapter on *Crusoe* as a myth of capitalism. It is not really relevant to argue, as critics of Watt have done, that Crusoe has little of the rational calculation of the capitalist. For Watt's point is that the book is a myth and not a literal picture, reflecting the dynamic spirit of capitalism rather than its practical application. "Crusoe's 'original sin' is really the dynamic tendency of capitalism itself, whose aim is never merely to maintain the *status quo,* but to transform it incessantly. Leaving home, improving on the lot one was born to, is a vital feature of the individualist pattern of life." The island permits individualism, and to imagine a Puritan Eden in which work yields gratification instead of vexation and defeat.

The special status of the island makes possible Crusoe's reaction, in a famous passage, when he finds a quantity of coins on board the wrecked ship.

> I smiled to myself at the sight of this money; "O drug!" said I aloud, "What art thou good for? Thou art not worth to me, no not the taking off of the ground, one of those

knives is worth all this heap, I have no manner of use for
thee, e'en remain where thou art, and go to the bottom as
a creature whose life is not worth saving." However, upon
second thoughts, I took it away.

Ever since Coleridge, readers have perceived irony in those second
thoughts, but the irony is at society's expense rather than Crusoe's.
If ever he returns to the world whose lifeblood is money, then this
money will be useful if not indispensable. With his usual good sense
he therefore saves it. But on the island, as if by enchantment, money
is truly valueless, and Crusoe is free of the whole remorseless system
whose lubricant it is. His personification of the coins as a "creature"
carries its traditional Puritan meaning: all earthly things are "creatures" which the saint is to restrain himself from loving too much.
Only on Crusoe's island is it possible to despise money as a useless
and indeed harmful drug.

Crusoe is no anchorite. Things retain their value, and in pillag-
ing the ship he never repents the urge to accumulate. "I had the
biggest magazine of all kinds now that ever were laid up, I believe,
for one man, but I was not satisfied still." What matters now is use,
exactly as Crusoe indicates in the "O drug" passage, and as he confirms in a later reference to the saved-up coins: "If I had had the
drawer full of diamonds it had been the same case; and they had been
of no manner of value to me, because of no use." Crusoe notes about
his early voyages that since he was a gentleman, a person with money
but no skills, he was a mere passenger and could do nothing useful.
On the island he has to work with his hands, something no gentleman would do, and recovers the dignity of labor which his father's
"middle station" might have insulated him from. Just as money
becomes meaningless, labor becomes meaningful. "A man's labour,"
Hobbes says, "is a commodity exchangeable for benefit, as well as
any other thing." Marx was hardly the first to notice the joylessness
of work performed solely for what it can buy. On the island Crusoe
has no market in which to sell his labor, and bestows it either on
making things he really wants or as an end in itself. It may take him
forever to make a pot, but Franklin's maxim has no meaning here:
time is not money. Defoe was a speculator and middleman; Crusoe
literalizes the labor theory of value in a miniature world where spec-
ulation is impossible and the middleman does not exist.

Relating *Robinson Crusoe* to the myth of Mammon, Starr surveys writers who tried to reconcile Christ's injunction "Take no thought for the morrow" with the duty of labor by emphasizing that the labor must be performed in cooperation with Providence. On the island Crusoe need no longer attempt this difficult reconciliation, whereas capitalism, being rational, must always take thought for the morrow. Thus in sociological terms Crusoe escapes the prison of alienated labor, just as in religious terms he escapes the prison of guilt. He inhabits a little world where his tools and products fully embody his desires (or would if he could make ink) and where necessity authenticates his desires instead of punishing them. "The liberty of the individual," Freud says, "is no gift of civilization." It is Defoe's gift to Crusoe.

Yet even in the imagination, this dream of wholeness is at best provisional. The economic system, according to Weber, "is an immense cosmos into which the individual is born, and which presents itself to him, at least as an individual, as an unalterable order of things in which he must live." On the island Crusoe breaks free from that order, but in a deeper sense he has already internalized it, along with the religious order that undergirds it. What is possible finally is only a fantasy of escape, from desire as well as from civilization, that anticipates the poor man's reward in the New Testament.

> I looked now upon the world as a thing remote, which I had nothing to do with, no expectation from, and indeed no desires about: in a word, I had nothing indeed to do with it, nor was ever like to have; so I thought it looked as we may perhaps look upon it hereafter, *viz.* as a place I had lived in, but was come out of it; and well might I say, as Father Abraham to Dives, *Between me and thee is a great gulf fixed.*

In a wonderful poem called "Crusoe's Journal," to which this passage is given an epigraph, Derek Walcott sees Crusoe through Friday's eyes as an invader rather than a hermit, using the Word to colonize Friday's mind as well as his body.

> even the bare necessities
> of style are turned to use,
> like those plain iron tools he salvages
> from shipwreck, hewing a prose
> as odorous as raw wood to the adze;

out of such timbers
came our first book, our profane Genesis . . .
in a green world, one without metaphors;
like Christofer he bears
in speech mnemonic as a missionary's
the Word to savages,
its shape an earthen, water-bearing vessel's
whose sprinkling alters us
into good Fridays who recite His praise,
parroting our master's
style and voice, we make his language ours,
converted cannibals
we learn with him to eat the flesh of Christ.

The Augustan satirists mocked man's lust for money—Swift's Yahoos with their bright stones, Pope's India millionaires—but Defoe cannot step outside the system, can only transport it to an imaginary island where he no longer recognizes it. And the naiveté of the "natural" speech that Walcott exposes, so full of hidden assumptions and hidden metaphors, brings us back to the Puritan anxiety about fiction and truth which takes on special urgency in the early novel.

Realism, Invention, Fantasy

In a sense Defoe's realism is perfectly obvious. His characters have names and experiences like those of ordinary English people, and even in exotic circumstances they remain prosaically familiar. "Realism" in this minimal sense is simply a representation of experience and (especially) of material details that confirms a culture's sense of the way things are. It also implies a rejection of the more ostentatious devices of art, either because the writer cunningly wants to give an illusion of unmediated fact, or because he naively believes that facts can actually be unmediated. Haller says that "artless realism" characterizes Puritan autobiography, and Ortega provides a social context by remarking that "In epochs with two different types of art, one for minorities and one for the majority, the latter has always been realistic." Augustan satire, written very much for the cultivated minority, constantly made fun of the artless realism affected by the new novels. *Gulliver's Travels* is in part a parody of *Robinson Crusoe,* and Swift delighted in a bishop's solemn pronouncement that he "hardly believed a word of it."

Some of the critical ambiguities in Defoe's realism may be inevitable in any fiction that masquerades as nonfiction. Ralph Rader says of *Moll Flanders,* "Knowing it to be a fiction in *fact,* critics try to understand it as if it were a fiction in *form.*" Still, to turn from autobiography to the novel is to turn away from the Puritan tradition with its genuinely artless realism. A comitted Puritan had no use for fiction, despising it as a form of lying and as an inexcusable preoccupation with wordly things. This distrust of fiction was no temporary phase, but persisted long in the evangelical tradition. In her youth George Eliot wrote that novels were "pernicious," declaring that she would carry to her grave "the mental diseases with which they have contaminated me." It was not only a question of possible immorality in fiction, but also of the status of fictionality itself: "Have I . . . any time to spend on things that never existed?"

Defoe was well aware of such objections, and by stressing his allegorical intentions he did his best to counter them. But more deeply, I believe, he opposed them not only because he thought Puritan faith compatible with fiction, but also because he was moved to test Puritan faith *through* fiction. To write novels, with however didactic an intention, was a subversive innovation. Insofar as Puritanism does indeed contribute to the rise of the novel, it is a case of the storytelling impulse asserting itself against the strongest possible inhibitions. So the mimetic realism that Watt stresses can be seen as a kind of mask to cover up what is actually happening: if the story can be presented *as* true, then it is less dreadful that it is *not* true. The author knows that it is fiction but the reader pretends not to, and so is not hurt by it—one is encouraged to read it in the same way, and with the same rewards, as one would read a true story.

Conversely, criticism's passion for detecting and analyzing the stratagems of art is a direct violation of the demands that such a novel makes, as Macaulay remarks in contrasting adult and childhood reading of *Robinson Crusoe*:

> He perceives the hand of a master in ten thousand touches which formerly he passed by without notice. But, though he understands the merits of the narrative better than formerly, he is far less interested by it. Xury and Friday, and pretty Poll, the boat with the shoulder-of-mutton sail, and the canoe which could not be brought down to the water edge, the tent with its hedge and ladders, the preserve of

kids, and the den where the goat died, can never again be
to him the realities which they were. . . . We cannot sit at
once in the front of the stage and behind the scenes. We
cannot be under the illusion of the spectacle while we are
watching the movements of the ropes and pulleys which
dispose it.

To some extent we must simply accept the fact that criticism is an
anesthetic (and often a contraceptive). But beyond this, Defoe's kind
of realism repels criticism because the pretense of *not* inventing reflects an emotional need, not just a novelistic program, which he
does his best to protect by concealing it from view. Fielding ostentatiously shows us the ropes and pulleys, but Defoe pretends they do
not exist.

What complicates matters profoundly is the commitment of
Puritan autobiography to faithfully reporting the "dealings" of God
with his creatures. By making up Crusoe and his adventures Defoe
unavoidably becomes the shaping diety of the narrative, and as Homer
Brown says,

The "real" self of Defoe's various "memoirs" is a fictive
self. Defoe's confessions are not *his* confessions at all. The
pattern of Christian truth has become the design of a lie
masked as actuality, the plot of a novel. . . . While Defoe
is impersonating Robinson Crusoe, he is also impersonating on another level Providence itself.

Hesitating in retrospect between incompatible ways of presenting his
work, Defoe claims that "the story, though allegorical, is also historical." At one moment he will imply that the island is an extended
metaphor: "It is as reasonable to represent one kind of imprisonment
by another, as it is to represent anything that really exists by that
which exists not." But at another moment he will claim that it is all
literally true: "It is most real that I had a parrot and taught it to call
me by my name; such a servant a savage, and afterwards a Christian,
and that his name was called Friday." In the preface to the novel itself
Defoe says with superb equivocation, "The editor believes the thing
to be a just history of fact; neither is there any appearance of fiction
in it."

The issue is not, as it was for Sidney, the philosophical legitimacy of fiction, but rather the dilemma incurred by a narrative that

claims to confirm religious faith by showing what really occurs rather than what an author might wish. This was not a serious problem for Bunyan, who could meet the charge of fictiveness by reminding the reader that *The Pilgrim's Progress* is only a dream and that it demands interpretation. Defoe is not prepared to make such an admission, which would explode the evidentiary claims of his tale. It was usual in Puritan biographies to marvel at a recurrence of significant dates that proved God's secret management of a person's life. Much is made of this in *Robinson Crusoe*. But the coincidence can only seem compelling if we are able to forget that Defoe, not God, has planted them in story.

Consider the early episode in which Crusoe escapes from slavery in North Africa. First of all Defoe gets him out to sea in a boat built by an English carpenter in a land without Englishman. On page 19 Crusoe says he had no fellow Englishman to talk with; on page 20 the carpenter "also was an English slave"; and on page 24 we learn that the boy Xury picked up his English "by conversing among us slaves," which makes it appear that there were several Englishmen. Presumably the carpenter occurred to Defoe for purely practical reasons—a native boat might go belly up whereas a stout English craft would not—but this indifference to consistency suggests that his freewheeling imagination is not tied down to narrow verisimilitude.

Once Crusoe is at sea Defoe still faces a minor annoyance. He can let Xury accompany Crusoe, but he must find some way to get rid of an adult Moor who is bound to cause trouble if he stays.

> Giving the boy the helm, I stepped forward to where the Moor was, and making as if I stooped for something behind him, I took him by surprise with my arm under his twist [crotch], and tossed him clear overboard into the sea; he rose immediately, for he swam like a cork, and called to me, begged to be taken in, told me he would go all over the world with me; he swam so strong after the boat that he would have reached me very quickly, there being but little wind; upon which I stepped into the cabin, and fetching one of the fowling-pieces I presented it at him, and told him I had done him no hurt, and if he would be quiet I would do him none; "But," said I, "you swim well enough to reach the shore, and the sea is calm, make the best of your way to shore and I will do you no harm, but if you

come near the boat I'll shoot you through the head, for I
am resolved to have my liberty;" so he turned himself
about and swam for the shore, and I make no doubt but he
reached it with ease, for he was an excellent swimmer.

In its leisurely unfolding this long sentence conceals important questions. Why was there a Moorish slave at all? Because it is implausible
that Crusoe would be allowed to go fishing with no companion but
a boy. Why does the man swim like a fish? Because Defoe wants no
blood on Crusoe's hands. The whole incident seems contrived to
give Crusoe a chance not to be guilty, allowing us as usual to focus
on his cleverness as a problem-solver rather than on his alleged in-
iquity as a sinner.

Defoe's contemporary Charles Gildon makes a penetrating re-
mark: "Though he afterwards proves so scrupulous about falling
upon the cannibals or men-eaters, yet he neither then nor afterwards
found any check of conscience in that infamous trade of buying and
selling men for slaves; else one would have expected him to have
attributed his shipwreck to this very cause." If this criticism had
seemed relevant to Defoe he would have dealt with it not by making
Crusoe feel guilty but by revising the story to leave out the slaves. In
point of fact Defoe supported the slave trade without reservation and
regarded the exploitation of slaves as a sign of business ability. When
Xury in his turn ceases to be useful Crusoe cheerfully sells him into
new slavery, an action that has scandalized many readers. But Defoe
seems not to worry about it; Xury is willing, and we hear of him no
more.

If Crusoe's island were really a scene of deserved punishment, it
would have been easy to have burdened him with punishable crimes.
He might have shot the cannibals, or at the very least the Moor
might have drowned. But Defoe as creator is never able to work for
long in harness with Defoe as homilist, not because his faith is hyp-
ocritical but because he cannot resist exploiting its inner tensions and
forcing both guilt and determinism to gratify desire instead of op-
posing it. The autobiographical genre, far from encouraging confessional introspection, liberates Defoe to share in what Richetti calls
"Crusoe's serene omnicompetence," giving embodied form to whatever he likes to imagine. Looking for a creek to land his raft in,
Crusoe duly finds a creek, and comments splendidly. "As I imagined, so it was."

Ricoeur summarizes Freud's theory of art in terms that have suggestive affinities with Defoe's fantasy of kingship and freedom:

> The artist, like the neurotic, is a man who turns away from reality because he cannot come to terms with the renunciation of instinctual satisfaction that reality demands, and who transposes his erotic and ambitious desires to the plane of fantasy and play. By means of his special gifts, however, he finds a way back to reality from this world of fantasy: he creates a new reality, the work of art, in which he himself becomes the hero, the king, the creator he desired to be, without having to follow the roundabout path of making real alterations in the external world.

Moreover, the apparently artless naiveté of first-person narration permits Defoe to bypass the external world even while appearing to confirm its details with unblinking accuracy. The mimetic texture works to conceal the existence of fantasy, while the intermittent presence of pattern is explained by attributing it to God rather than to the novelist.

The fantasy, incidentally, is comprehensive enough to shift from a solitary to a political form, and not just in the obvious sense that Crusoe colonizes Friday. The twenty-eight years of Crusoe's exile coincide with the period from the fall of Puritan rule in 1660 to the overthrow of the Catholic James II in 1688—and by a happy coincidence these were the first twenty-eight years of Defoe's life. So Crusoe enjoys an exile that is also an assertion of hidden authority, commensurate with the underground status of Puritanism during those years. And then suddenly he becomes absolute sovereign over a mixed polity consisting of cannibals, Spaniards, and Englishmen; the childhood fantasy of mastery over an unpeopled world is succeeded by an adolescent fantasy of mastery over other men (women do not appear on the island until the *Farther Adventures*). Perhaps this is a last expression of Puritan wish-fulfillment in the political realm, a fantasy revenge for the disappointments of the Glorious Revolution of 1688 as well as for the bitterness of the Restoration of 1660.

There are further paradoxes in a desert-island realism. The book is realistic in lovingly presenting a wealth of miscellaneous details, but is remote from any evocation of a social reality. J. P. Stern's treatment of this kind of exceptional case is helpful:

> May not a special plea on behalf of a single man's experience be true? It *is* true, so long as it remains special: so long as it is offered as a single man's experience. Its characteristic form of expression is lyrical poetry. It becomes available to realism only at the point where the experience is worsted in the disillusioning conflict with the world of other people.

This is why I argued at the outset of this study that Lukács is right: a strong lyric impulse underlies the earliest novels. Crusoe redefines (or perhaps escapes) the disillusioning world of other people, and elaborates a seemingly realistic world out of the private experience of one man. Among the many possible reasons why Defoe's later novels are inferior to *Robinson Crusoe*, an essential one is their failure to recapture this dream in the midst of society.

Yet *Robinson Crusoe* is no lyric poem, and it is equally important to remember how consistently it refuses to let us see *into* Crusoe, defining his experience instead as a series of reactions to outward objects. "I carried two hatchets to try if I could not cut a piece off of the roll of lead, by placing the edge of one hatchet and driving it with the other; but as it lay about a foot and a half in the water, I could not make any blow to drive the hatchet." Anyone who has tried to strike a blow under water must feel the rightness of this, and it thus achieves its purpose of making one feel that it must be true: if it had not happened, who would think to make it up? But Defoe did make it up, and the outwardness of *Crusoe* is an inverted mask for the inwardness of Defoe.

Allegory and mimesis are both, in the end, cover stories for the unacknowledged fantasy. But critics interested in Defoe's religious and economic ideas have tended to take his "realism" at face value, giving insufficient attention to the extraordinary extent of narcissistic wish-fulfillment in *Robinson Crusoe*. In this light Marthe Robert's analysis is deeply interesting, whether or not one wants to adopt the psychoanalytic explanation that she uses to organize her insights. As the title of her book makes clear—*Roman des Origines et Origine du Roman*—she identifies the origin of the novel/romance with the Freudian "family romance" in which the child imagines its own origin. *Robinson Crusoe* is for Robert the prime example of the foundling fantasy in which the child repudiates its parents, dreams of nobler and more powerful ones to whom it actually belongs, and elaborates a dream of omnipotence in a paradisal world undisturbed by other people and (especially) by sexuality. "Having wished to be nobody's son [Crusoe] becomes in fact completely orphaned, completely alone, the innocent self-begetter in a kingdom of complete solitude." Reborn from the sea after the shipwreck—many critics have noticed the birth imagery as he struggles ashore—Crusoe enters an ambiguous Eden that expresses, but cannot reconcile, both the guilt that landed him there and the innocence that fantasy seeks to recreate. "He is unsure whether he is chosen or damned, miraculously taken to the heart of unsullied nature, or condemned to a hell of silence and oblivion."

In the extended "apprenticeship to reality" that follows this rebirth, Crusoe recapitulates civilization's growth to maturity, reinventing its arts and ideas (including a naive version of theology) and reaching the point where he can become a surrogate father to Friday, guardian of other castaways, and emperor of his little kingdom. But of course this is still very much a dream of omnipotence, however disguised as realism, and Robert sees the realistic novel's repudiation of mere "art" as reflecting its achievement in accommodating fantasy to the world of experience. "Unlike all other representational genres the novel is never content to *represent* but aims rather at giving a 'complete and genuine' account of everything, as if, owing to some special dispensation or magic power, it had an unmediated contact with reality." A fantasy of innocent gratification is put forward as being perfectly consistent with the reality principle. And Defoe's dogged defense of the new realism, naive though it may seem to later critical theory, exactly captures that sense of magically unmediated truth that Robert describes. Puritan writers in earlier generations had aspired to unmediated contact with God, but had recognized that all human expression is necessarily mediated through emblem and type (which is what makes them in a certain sense seem "modern" today). In Defoe's world the divine recedes ever farther away into the remote heavens, ceasing to be the essential guarantor of understanding, and the symbols he inherits from Puritanism are now free to assert their independent reality.

If the Puritans believed that they had to study the clues in their lives with fierce attention, they also believed that the ultimate interpretation was reserved for God, not themselves. "In theistic religions," Frye says, "God speaks and man listens." But in *Robinson Crusoe* God himself becomes a kind of fiction, even if an indispensable one, and Crusoe has to do his own interpreting because if he does not, no one else will. *Paradise Lost* and *The Pilgrim's Progress* were texts that depended upon a superior text, the Word of God. *Robinson Crusoe* contains plenty of scriptural allusions, but now they are only allusions. The narrative offers itself as autonomous and freestanding, and in a profound sense it is secular. Here is where the "realism" of Crusoe telling his own story conflicts with the impulse to interpret, and the story tends to roll onward with a momentum of its own rather than successfully embodying the pattern to which it aspires. Crusoe is moved by his father's advice "but alas! a few days wore it all off," and this sets the tone for everything that follows. In a way Defoe participates in the state of continuous starting-over that is characteristic of modern writing, "something whose *beginning* condition, irreducibly, is that *it must always be produced, constantly.*" So in a curious way Defoe's problems lead logically to the solutions of Sterne, who perfectly fulfills Barthes's definition, "Le texte scriptible, c'est *nous en train* d'écrire." But one must not claim too much; *Robinson Crusoe* resists any theoretical explanation that sees its meanderings as planned. A recent writer proposes, modestly enough, that "there is a deliberate avoidance of rhetorical or dramatic closure in Defoe's method." The impersonal and passive construction is all too apt: the method itself (not Defoe) does not want to end, and the avoidance of ending is somehow "in" the method.

If Crusoe watches himself writing, Defoe pretends to watch neither Crusoe nor himself, affecting an utterly unsubordinated prose whose heaped up clauses suggest the mind-numbing inconsequentiality of experience. Here is the first half of a typical sentence, with the connective words italicized for emphasis:

> A little after noon I found the sea very calm, *and* the tide ebbed so far out, *that* I could come within a quarter of a mile of the ship; *and* here I found a fresh renewing of my grief, *for* I saw evidently, *that* if we had kept on board, we had all been safe, *that is to say,* we had all got safe on shore, *and* I had not been so miserable *as* to be left entirely destitute of all comfort and company, *as* I now was; *this* forced tears from my eyes again, *but* as there was little relief in that, I resolved, *if* possible, to get to the ship, *so* I pulled off my clothes, *for* the weather was hot to extremity, *and* took the water, *but* when I came to the ship, my difficulty was

still greater to know how to get on board, *for* as she lay aground.

In Bunyan the paratactic style suggested the welter of experience that God pulls together into a single shape. In Defoe it just suggests the welter of experience, and the prose keeps toppling forward of its own weight.

Christian faith is well on the way to providing a nostalgic schema rather than an informing principle, even if as Lukács says it has left permanent scars on the landscape: "The river beds, now dry beyond all hope, have marked forever the face of the earth." Defoe's later novels are exceptionally episodic, not only failing to make their inner logic conform to providential plan, but failing to develop an inner logic at all. And the anomie that *Robinson Crusoe* held at bay returns with a vengeance. The later characters live under aliases while struggling, usually as criminals, to survive in a society that offers no *nomos,* no status that confirms the essential order of things. And guilt is no longer managed by assimilating it to a coherent determinism generated from within. Moll Flanders's rationalizations may be partly shared by the author, but he certainly appreciates the dreadful emptiness (and Pauline urgency) in Roxana's bitter confession: "With my eyes open, and with my conscience, as I may say, awake, I sinned, knowing it to be a sin, but having no power to resist." We cannot know exactly what Defoe thought he was doing in this enigmatic novel, but we do know that it was his last. As one critic puts it, "Defoe stopped when he reached the end."

Meanwhile *Robinson Crusoe* survives in all its richness, the starting point of a new genre and yet strangely unfruitful for imitation; it spawned no tradition of its own as *Don Quixote* and *Pamela* did. Later fictions continued to draw upon Christian ideas and to pursue the dream of confirming them, but never again in the naive and direct way that Defoe at first believed possible. *Robinson Crusoe* is a remarkable and unrepeatable reconciliation of myth with novel, whose fantasy of isolation without misery and labor without alienation retains all of its remarkable imaginative power. "I am away from home," Kafka wrote to his closest friend, "and must always write home, even if any home of mine has long since floated away into eternity. All this writing is nothing but Robinson Crusoe's flag hoisted at the highest point of the island."

Crusoe's Island Exile

Michael Seidel

In *Ulysses,* Leopold Bloom, the Irish Odysseus, poses an exile's question to another exile whom Joyce called the English Ulysses: *"O, poor Robinson Crusoe! / How could you possibly do so?"* Bloom's lilting refrain comes from a popular turn-of-the-century song that recalls a haunting moment in *Robinson Crusoe* when Defoe's castaway, alone at that time for six years, hears the disembodied voice of his previously trained wild parrot, Poll, ask, *"Robin, Robin, Robin Crusoe,* poor *Robin Crusoe,* where are you *Robin Crusoe?* Where are you? Where have you been?"

Before Crusoe was startled by the parrot's words he had been on a reconnaissance mission, or *periplous* sailing around part of his island in a small canoe, or *periagua.* He had almost been carried beyond the island by ocean currents, at which point he looked back on the place of his exile as a kind of paradisiac home.

> Now I look'd back upon my desolate solitary Island, as the most pleasant Place in the World, and all the happiness my Heart could wish for, was to be but there again. I stretch'd out my Hands to it with eager Wishes. O happy Desart, said I, I shall never see thee more. O miserable Creature, said I, whither am I going: Then I reproach'd my self with my unthankful Temper, and how I had repin'd at my

From *Exile and the Narrative Imagination.* ©1986 by Yale University. Yale University Press, 1986.

solitary Condition; and now what would I give to be on Shore there again. Thus we never see the true State of our Condition, till it is illustrated to us by its Contraries; nor know how to value what we enjoy, but by the want of it.

Exile for Crusoe is now anywhere *but* his island, including the great sea whence he came. Fortunately, he negotiates the treacherous currents, beaches the canoe, and heads on foot toward his inland bower, or country house, for a miniature homecoming of sorts. His trek exhausts him, and he is half asleep when he hears the parrot's baffling questions. Poll, having flown in on its own accord from Crusoe's seaward settlement, chooses this occasion to repeat, by imprint, the sounds it has recorded during the early, more trying years of Crusoe's exile. So in the same sense that a loner's experience is rather like talking to other versions of himself, the questions the parrot asks of Crusoe are the same as those asked earlier by Crusoe. The questions themselves possess a double structure, hinting at two times and two places, at the Crusoe who hears them (where *are* you?) and the Crusoe who asked them (where have you *been?*). The exile faces the dilemma that he is, indeed, of two places. Or, to put it another way, where he is displaced becomes his home place. Paradoxically, the answers to both the parrot's questions are in a generic sense the same: home. Home is where Crusoe now is, and home is where he had been. It is as Elizabeth Bishop puts it in her poem, "Crusoe in England": "Home-made, home-made! But aren't we all?"

Crusoe himself recognizes the mental and territorial transformation when he comments much earlier on the first night he ever spent away from his original settlement, the seaward hutch, after exploring the inland savannas: "I spent all that Evening there, and went not back to my Habitation, which by the Way was the first Night, as I might say, I had lain from Home." The locution "as I might say" makes the condition figurative but no less real for Crusoe in exile. Several months later, he undertakes an exploration of the island by foot and, after about thirty days, gets homesick.

I cannot express what a Satisfaction it was to me, to come into my old Hutch, and lye down in my Hamock-Bed: This little wandring Journey, without settled Place of Abode, had been so unpleasant to me, that my own House, as I call'd it to my self, was a perfect Settlement to me, compar'd to that; and it rendred every Thing about me so comfortable, that I resolv'd I would never go a great Way from it again, while it should be my Lot to stay on the Island.

Of course, it is in Crusoe's wandering nature to abjure this particular promise or any like it upon the shortest possible notice, but of more immediate interest is the psychological appropriation of exilic space entailed by his coming "home." Crusoe refers to his island exile as "my Reign, or my Captivity, which you please." By whatever principle of abundant or redundant locution we do please, that place from which the exile is blocked becomes the model for the place in which he resettles his imagination. Crusoe's habit of mind has been "made" permanently binary, a process or, more accurately, a figuration represented in Crusoe's ledger "Accompt," where the tension between the anxieties of separation and the activities of resettlement are represented in graphic (or written) shape in double columns on the page. He records on the side of separation: *"I am divided from Mankind, a Solitaire, one banish'd from humane Society"*; and on the side of resettlement (in every sense): *"But I am not starv'd and perishing on a barren Place, affording no Sustenance."* Crusoe's ledger conforms to his condition as exile: displacement and replacement are something of the same phenomenon.

The way Crusoe thinks in exile effects the way Defoe writes him up. Language mimics perception as the horror of isolation turns into the relief of deliverance: "as my Life was a Life of Sorrow, one way, so it was a Life of Mercy, another." Crusoe's way of articulating his condition reinforces the pattern that courses through the entire narrative, the double-entry accounting that transvalues experience. In his initial despair, Crusoe's hutch was but a hovel. Later, in full pride of place, his shelter becomes an estate; his estate, a kingdom; his kingdom, a paradise. When, and for whatever reasons, Crusoe's insecurities return, his paradise shrinks to his cave. If he feels fearful or hostile, his cave becomes his fortification. Crusoe's exile is an invitation to conversion, not simply a turning or movement from place to place but a transformation—imaginative and psychological—of one place or state of mind *into* another. This is, of course, also at the heart of the fictional record that makes up his exilic story.

"My Brain Bred Islands"

It is precisely the exilic doubleness of Crusoe's situation or placement that accounts for the generative and allegorical texture of the narrative. When Defoe got around to commenting, seriously or otherwise, on his fictional strategies in *Crusoe,* he recognized that, however great his urge to substantiate a particular story, any sequence of narrative carries with it the pattern for interchangeability or duplication. Such a notion finds its way into the text of *Robinson Crusoe,* and Crusoe himself articulates it on his Brazilian plantation before he had any way of knowing about his subsequent island exile: "I used to say, I liv'd just like a Man cast away upon some desolate island, that had no body there but himself." Crusoe points out that those who utter such words may have heaven "oblige them to make the Exchange." Indeed, both heaven and Defoe so oblige.

Defoe writes at greater length of narrative interchangeability in his extended commentary on the story of the exiled Crusoe, *Serious Reflections during the Life and Surprizing Adventures of Robinson Crusoe* (1720). His voice is nominally that of Crusoe as a fictional being but actually that of himself as an authorial being: "In a word, there is not a circumstance in the imaginary story but has its just allusion to a real story, and chimes part for part and step for step with the inimitable Life of Robinson Crusoe." Defoe cites as an example of what he means an illustration chosen not from the original narrative but from a later section of *Serious Reflections.*

> For example, in the latter part of this work called the Vision, I begin thus: "When I was in my island-kingdom I had abundance of strange notions of my seeing apparitions," &c. All these reflections are just history of a state of forced confinement, which in my real history is represented by a confined retreat in an island; and it is as reasonable to represent one kind of imprisonment by another, as it is to represent any thing that really exists by that which exists not.

Fable achieves a kind of reality by calling to mind replicative sets of experience. "My brain bred islands," as Bishop puts it in "Crusoe in England." In *Serious Reflections,* Defoe makes a claim for what he calls the allegorical historical method of narration while defending himself (in the guise of Crusoe) from those who have charged him with lying.

> I Robinson Crusoe, being at this Time in perfect and sound mind and memory, thanks be to God therefor, do hereby declare their objection is an invention scandalous in design, and false in fact; and do affirm that the story, though allegorical, is also historical; and that it is the beautiful representation of a life of unexampled misfortunes, and of a variety not to be met with in the world, sincerely adapted to and intended for the common good of mankind, and designed first, as it is now farther applied, to the most serious uses possible.

Defoe writes in Crusoe's name but leaves the possibility open that what is described as Crusoe's life happened to someone else: Crusoe's story is the fabrication of other "real" events. This much is, at least, half true. Crusoe's story is a fabrication. Defoe, still in Crusoe's voice, suggests that the process of reading is naturally allegorical—that the mind makes one thing stand for comparable things no matter what the real or invented status of the events narrated. In essence, Defoe is trying very hard to shift the grounds of the argument surrounding fictional invention from verifiability to application. Now we have before us the possibility that the island adventure did not take place but that its writing makes it real for those reading it. The book is, after all, read and experienced. Its contents empty into one's brain. Crusoe had less wittingly already offered a similar argument during his actual island adventure when, after an ague-inspired vision, he saw before him a terrifying Avenging Angel: "No one, that shall ever read this Account, will expect that I should be able to describe the Horrors of my Soul at this terrible Vision, I mean, that even while it was a Dream, I even dreamed of those Horrors; nor is it any more possible to describe the impression that remain'd upon my Mind when I awak'd and found it was but a Dream." The phrase "that even while it was a Dream, I even dreamed of those Horrors" can mean only that the unreal action of dream *as dream* left a real impression. On just such terms would Defoe defend the validity of fictional event as "real." It is *made* real to the reader and therefore takes on tangible status in regard to the uses to which it might be put.

"There are a great many sorts of those people who make it their business to go about telling stories," Defoe writes in *Serious Reflections*. Among them are those who, out of the forge of invention, "hammer out the very person, man or woman, and begin, 'I knew the man,' or 'I knew the woman.' " But the

> selling or writing a parable or an allusive allegoric history, is quite a different case, and is always distinguished from this other jesting with truth, that it is designed and effec- tually turned for instructive and upright ends, and has its moral justly applied. Such are the historical parables in the Holy Scripture, such "The Pilgrim's Progress," and such, in a word, the adventures of your fugitive friend, "Robinson Crusoe."

Once relieved of justifying fiction merely by verifying the oc- currence of its events, it becomes possible for Defoe to encourage his readers to think about the significance and design of events relayed as narrative sequence, so that, for example, a reader might expand allegorically upon the idea of solitude from that "which I have rep- resented to the world, and of which you must have formed some ideas from the life of a man in an island." As Defoe writes in another context: "Things seem to appear more lively to the Understanding, and to make a stronger Impression upon the Mind, when they are insinuated under the cover of some Symbol or Allegory, especially when the Moral is good, and the Application easy." Allegory always represents one thing *in* another, and this representation, as we have seen, is very close to what the word *allegory* means: a speaking oth- erwise where difference itself becomes a form of duplication. Crusoe is more conscious than most fictional characters that an allegory of one kind or another has been going on around him. He even begins a journal that repeats the allegorical shape of the adventure he is in by mirroring its key word and recurrent theme, deliverance, in terms of his impulse to write it up. He writes, as he puts it, in order to "deliver my Thoughts from daily poring upon them, and afflicting my Mind."

Defoe understands that writing serves to intensify action, imbue it with calculated strangeness, remoteness, liminality that engages as it expands one's interest. The adventures of Crusoe in the original volume are both *Strange* and *Surprizing*. In *Serious Reflections,* Defoe as Crusoe—or Crusoe as Defoe—compares himself to "the teacher, like a greater [Christ], having no honour in his own country." Such a teacher knows that "Facts that are formed to touch the mind, must be done a great way off, and by somebody never heard of." Familiarity breeds contempt; strangeness or remoteness attracts attention. Crusoe hedges a bit as to whether the adventures he has experienced happened where he represented them, on an island near the mouth of the Orinoco, or somewhere much closer to home. Having raised the allegorical stakes, Defoe wonders whether his readers would lose interest "when you are supposing the scene, which is placed so far off, had its original so near home?" The question comports with Defoe's notion that a unique metaphoric configuration makes a greater impression on the mind than a familiar literal one, but it also opens up the territory of the imagination as an exilic supplement.

Home, of course, is a key word in the text of *Crusoe* itself and around it is organized the potential for allegory. To strike home is to startle into realization: "The world, I say, is nothing to us, but as it is more or less to our relish. All reflection is carried home, and our dear self is, in one respect, the end of living." The self-discovery that is the object of the interpreting mind is imaged constantly in the allegorical discovery that takes place in the sequence of narrative duplications. The allegorical self is a homebody. Crusoe's discovery of an old goat in his cave is perhaps an apposite example. He need not even know exactly what he means when he says it, but when he comes upon the goat he comes upon Crusoe allegorized: "I durst to believe there was nothing in this Cave that was more frightful than my self." Crusoe in exile is always discovering himself.

In a more general sense, ten months into his stay Crusoe hits upon the principle that rules the narrative: "Having now secur'd my Habitation, as I thought, fully to my Mind, I had a great Desire to make a more perfect Discovery of the Island, and to see what other Productions I might find, which I yet knew nothing of." This not only repeats the central pattern of action, the narrative and psychological temptation to enlarge the perimeters of experience, but it provides a resource for the analyzing, performing, and, in the final analysis, the imagining mind. It is as "Discovery" that the status of the island encourages the generous range of allegorical propensities that seem given over to it. The island is located in the fantasy of its own sovereign imagining, that "true" space, as Melville says of Queequeg's island in *Moby-Dick,* that "is not down in any map; true places never are." Elizabeth Bishop's "Crusoe in England" makes the same point.

but my poor old island's still
un-rediscovered, un-renamable.
None of the books has ever got it right.

Robinson Crusoe is the only book that does get it right. It pro-
liferates meaning from its island exile: linguistic, temporal, psychological, spiritual, political. Crusoe himself participates in and
encourages the process, reading and misreading the nature of his
experience, supplementing his adventure by creating other versions
of it that, in narrative terms, never happened: "I spent whole Hours,
I may say whole Days, in representing to my self in the most lively
Colours, how I must have acted, if I had got nothing out of the Ship.
How I could not have so much as got any Food, except Fish and
Turtles; and that as it was long before I found any of them, I must
have perish'd first. That I should have liv'd, if I Had not perish'd,
like a meer Savage." Robinson Crusoe's story is so allegorically
bountiful that it supplements its own island supplement.

"WHY DID YOU LEAVE YOUR FATHER'S HOUSE?"
"TO SEEK MISFORTUNE."

Defoe does not presume a single, privileged allegorical reading
for Crusoe's adventures at the expense of the narrative's general
power as a saga of adaptation and endurance, as a study of isolation
and fear, and as a tale of the mobile fantasy and transforming imagination. But from the beginning of the action it seems clear that the
pattern of separation and exile is at the heart of the narrative no
matter how we would read it, and that the initiating event of all the
action, Crusoe's disobedience to the wishes of his father that he stay
at home, is complexly implicated in the run of the adventure abroad.

Crusoe steadfastly disobeys despite, perhaps even because of,
his father's proposal to settle him: "In a word, that as he would do
very kind things for me if I would stay and settle at Home as he
directed, so he would not have so much hand in my Misfortunes, as
to give me any Encouragement to go away." Every word here is
rich, from the hint of originating authority, the "word," to the
countercommand of adventure, "stay," to the multivalent "settle,"
to the allegorical "Home," to the archetypal "Misfortunes." The last
plays on the paradigm of the prodigal son as Joyce plays on it in
Ulysses—leaving the father's land or motherland "to seek misfor-
tune"—and becomes the essence of exilic alienation.

In one sense, perhaps a political one, Crusoe's spirit during his years of exile represents the antithesis to patriarchal home rule; in another, Crusoe's anguish at his original disobedience (he calls it his original sin) is genuine, though most severe when he feels least secure. Crusoe never does quite sort out the difference in motive between sin and impulse, and the question for the narrative action is whether resistance to his father's demands serves him better than had he succumbed to them. Crusoe is positioned so that his initial resistance to his home is the prelude to a crisis or series of crises that are themselves steps in a process of self-substantiation and return. The measure of Crusoe's hard-won settlement is the degree to which his impulses force him to avoid too easy a settlement too soon. This process, I will later argue, provides the political basis of the narrative's exilic structure. Crusoe's father's advice has to be tempered by the exclusionary nature of its focus. Some obvious courses of action cost more in anguish to follow than to resist, and there are times when the secure and complacent life he recommends is worse than the necessary errantry of a liberated soul. "I broke loose," Crusoe says of his initial sea voyage, and he is always doing so. His island exile is the final project of his "rambling Designs."

At one point in the *Farther Adventures of Robinson Crusoe,* a merchant in the Bay of Bengal tries to talk Crusoe into a sailing expedition. His argument reflects back on the initiating scene of the first volume: "For what should we stand still for? The whole world is in motion, rolling round and round; all the creatures of God, heavenly bodies and earthly, are busy and diligent, why should we be idle?" The notion of rootedness is associated with the buzzword *idleness.* Defoe's narratives count on the principle of mobility, self-propulsion, and self-extension. Motion is fate. Near the beginning of Defoe's *Memoirs of a Cavalier,* the hero's mother dreams that she wanders out into the middle of a field in order to give birth to a son who, in half an hour's time, sprouts a pair of wings and flies away. The incipient cavalier is dreamed up as one of narrative's bird signs; his is an inborn tendency to fly the coop. As is the case for Crusoe's "wandring Inclination," the cavalier has elsewhere built into his nature.

Defoe's fiction gains its power by playing the mobile self off the desiring self. Moll Flanders, for example, whose mobility is class-inspired, and whose energies are sexually keen—a better word might be *smart*—seeks the security of the sobriquet *gentlewoman,* but finds herself removed to the very borders of the English-speaking world in America to attain it. Moll tests the status of gentility, which she seems to think means enterprising but which her first employer knew meant flesh peddling, with a set of prodigal relations in Virgina. Because of the exigencies of bourgeois fate, her new husband turns out to be her brother, and her mother-in-law her mother *in deed.* If on Crusoe's faraway island the values of hard-won sovereignty come up against the threat of cannibalism, in *Moll Flanders* newfangled gentility contests with a primordial taboo, incest. Moll's New World interlude is a paradigm of limits; it sets the contours of activity not merely in the simple sense of casting a character to the extremes but in the more complex sense of reaccommodating that character to his or her sense of center once the extremes are subsumed as part of experience. The mobile fantasy entails negotiation at the boundary between extreme circumstance and the formation of character. Usually, matters are turned to profit. As appalled as Moll was at what she called her undoing in Virginia, her brother/husband's estate eventually stakes her future. By the end of the narrative she literally "capitalizes" the incest taboo, which works for her the way Crusoe's Brazilian plantation worked for him as a land bank in exile.

The voyage out for Defoe is the sovereignty the self establishes over contingency. This is part of the reason that Crusoe first frames his "irresistible Reluctance . . . to going home" as a negative power: "I had several times loud Calls from my Reason and my more composed Judgment to go home, yet I had no Power to do it." He knows that settlement brings its own rewards, but he operates under a different imperative. Even when his reason tells him to stay put in Brazil and he is willing to admit, given his previous ill luck, that his voyaging scheme is "the most preposterous Thing that ever Man in such Circumstances could be guilty of," he feels compelled to undertake it. Later, when his rhetorical and religious guard is down on the island, he tells us what really drives him: "I seldom gave any Thing over without accomplishing it, when I once had it in my Head enough to begin it." He refers to his conviction that in time he would have figured a way to brew beer, but his sentiment applies to almost all his actions and it resides at the center of his sometimes mercurial character.

"Freedom Lives Hence, and Banishment Is Here"

When Defoe speaks, as he does at length in *Serious Reflections,* of Crusoe's adventure acting the role of allegory to bring the remote nearer home, he means by home any and all familiar mental territory. But he also has an exilic fable in mind that makes Crusoe's island, as a home away from home, politically allusive. Crusoe's displacement overlaps a time in English history near, if not dear, to Defoe's heart. It does not tax the imagination, beyond the levy Defoe has already allowed it, to consider the interplay between the narrative's temporal configuration and the fold of years "at home" that coincide with Crusoe's time on his island. Defoe placed Crusoe in "banishment," as he calls it, from 1659 to 1686 (he returns to England a year later in 1687), a period of twenty-eight years that virtually parallels the years of the Stuart Restoration in England. In a deliberate and calculated sense, Defoe makes of Crusoe's reign a government in exile.

For reasons that Defoe never forgot, the Stuart Restoration seemed apostolic to him. Crusoe is cast ashore on the island a year before the return of Charles II, and he does not set foot on English soil until over a quarter of a century later just as arrangements for the Williamite succession are under way, a succession that would follow a Glorious Revolution Defoe considered foundational. As is characteristic of the exilic reflex in narrative, Defoe represents on Crusoe's island an ideological supplement separated from home but effectively replacing the regime in power. Crusoe, without any real political awareness of his own, sustains, like so many exiles, the values of his original land during a time when that land seemed incapable, at least in Defoe's view, of sustaining them properly itself. Defoe felt about the Stuarts at home in England what Kent felt about Lear's daughters: "Freedom lives hence, and banishment is here" (1.1.180). Subsequently, just prior to the time James II and his Stuart supporters are exiled, Defoe ushers his island sovereign home to forecast England's renewed legitimacy or its return to its senses.

Again, I am making an argument not for Crusoe's awareness of the temporal politics of his exilic fable but for Defoe's. He felt that the important gap in the continuity of English history was not the dramatic parliamentary revolution from 1641 through the Cromwellian Protectorate but those alien years from 1660 to 1688, coincidental also with the first twenty-eight years of his own life, during which his family was victimized, at least early in the Restoration, by the oppressive Clarendon codes. *Robinson Crusoe* takes its place alongside traditional narratives where exilic duration is a kind of test until national history is, in a way, ready to legitimize itself. Individuals and peoples best represent themselves by metaphorically standing outside their land.

The Stuarts, in Defoe's view, had two-timed the home island, enshrined a legitimacy founded on worn-out principles of Divine Right and Passive Obedience, and secured the safety of the realm in its later years by the swiftness and exigency of the executioner's ax. It is possible to say that the Restoration, in which most of Defoe's narratives are set, is the epoch that most haunted his imagination, and the notion of the period as a kind of *trou*, lapse, or hiatus is not one to which Defoe turns for the first time in *Robinson Crusoe*. He began his career with a pamphlet attack on the Stuarts, and his major early works capped, so to speak, the alien politics of the previous century. *The Consolidator* (1705) and *Jure Divino* (1706) are both relentless, detailed indictments of Stuart tyranny. Defoe specifically called *The Consolidator*, his first sustained fictional narrative, an "allegorick Relation," and the action sets a lunar philosopher on the moon to talk out and act out the precepts of the 1688 Glorious Revolution while explicitly attacking "lunar" (or lunatic) politics, the much less glorious practices of the Stuart kings, or any who would follow Stuart policies into the eighteenth century.

From the beginning of his career, Defoe had a countermyth in mind, one that depicted the true course of English history not as passive obedience in the face of *jure divino* but as a project or speculative adventure. It is in this sense that many readers have intuited that Crusoe stands for something central in the English experience, even if he does so without a sense of national mission. His exile is a kind of blind trust, a metaphorical account that earns its interest not only as a new kind of sovereignty but as a new national enterprise. In his first full-length work in the 1690s, *Essay upon Projects*, Defoe offers up the Crusoe type and symbol in incipient form, the merchant adventurer with practical vision who, in the face of all manner of risk, is still "the most intelligent Man in the World, and consequently the most capable, when urg'd by Necessity, to Contrive New Ways to live." He repeats the essence of this notion much later in his career, after *Robinson Crusoe*, when he refers to the English merchant as a kind of cycle of redemption in and of himself, an allegory of risk, endurance, and profit: "The English tradesman is a kind of phoenix, who rises out of his own ashes, and makes the ruin of his fortunes be a firm foundation to build his recovery."

The inauguration of Crusoe's trials always involve risk devolving from capital venture. His island exile proper begins after several intervening commercial years that include imprisonment after capture by pirates and, upon his escape from North Africa, the establishment of a plantation in Brazil. Crusoe claims that setting up the plantation puts him in the same settled stay-at-home condition his father recommended to him "and which if I resolved to go on with, I might as well ha' staid at Home, and never have fatigu'd my self in the World as I had done." It is not so much Crusoe's conviction speaking here that events such as his earlier capture by the Moors, his escape to the African coast, and his hacking a plantation out of the wilds of South America are the equivalent of taking a law degree—to which his father was willing to stake him—as it is his conviction that he is destined for a more risk-filled life than he happens to be living at the time.

Crusoe departs Brazil September 1, 1659 and he comes to ruin on September 30, 1659. The prelude to his island adventure, as death stares him in the face aboard a foundering ship, previews the ultimate exilic fate, the crossing into another world: "In a word, we sat looking upon one another, and expecting Death every Moment, and every Man acting accordingly, as preparing for another World, for there was little or nothing more for us to do in this." Crusoe is thrust on his island, and his very survival is a rebirth into a new condition or "state," which seems to repeat the scene near the beginning of the narrative when the young Robinson swoons during his first shipwreck only to awake "with Horror of Mind and the Thoughts of what was yet before me." In this earlier scene the future plot of the whole plays out in its adverbial part; what is later "before" Crusoe after his second wreck is the battle for life that becomes his restoration.

> Nothing can describe the Confusion of Thought which I felt when I sunk into the Water; for tho' I swam very well, yet I could not deliver my self from the Waves so as to draw Breath, till that Wave having driven me, or rather carried me a vast Way on towards the Shore, and having

spent it self, went back, and left me upon the Land almost
dry, but half-dead with the Water I took in.

The sea comes at Crusoe, again as a landed form and then as an
enemy: "For I saw the Sea come after me as high as a great Hill, and
as furious as an Enemy which I had no Means or Strength to contend
with." Crusoe's business, at least in the metaphoric language with
which he relays his experience, is to serve as his own self-regulator
or governor: "[to] Pilot my self toward the Shore." Later, when the
wrecked ship appears for his salvaging and Crusoe loads a raft with
booty, he steers toward a cove near the mouth of an island creek to
moor his vessel and, in an almost symbolic gesture, marks his sovereignty by "sticking my two broken Oars into the Ground." When
he considers future trips to the wrecked ship for salvaging, his self-
sovereignty becomes participatory: "I call'd a Council, that is to say,
in my Thoughts." From disaster comes a plan, or council, for the
beginnings of a new order of things. Of course, if we credit the
possibility of a temporal juxtaposition with English home rule, we
also credit Crusoe's language of resettlement as conventional to a
fault. We have seen its metaphoric equivalent with every crucial
change of government in England, particularly with the host of en-
comia for the Stuart beachhead in 1660 that figure the return of
Charles II as the restoration of calm after a storm at sea. Dryden, for
example, compresses the king's exile and return in the following
lines:

> To all the Sea-Gods *Charles* an Off'ring owes:
> A Bull to thee *Portunus* shall be slain,
> A Lamb to you the Tempests of the Main:
> For those loud stormes that did against him rore
> Have cast his shipwrack'd Vessel on the shore.
> ("Astraea Redux," 11.120–24)

Defoe need not have remembered the specific Dryden passage
here—that is not the point I am making. What is significant is the
antithetical nature of Crusoe's beachhead in 1659; his new estate
signals what Defoe always believed, that the true Englishman was
compromised when the Stuarts were in his "home" and he was, so
to speak, "out of it." Restoration means resupply or restocking,
literally laying away for the future. Crusoe is as well established, in
this sense, as his temporal sovereign rival; in fact, one of the plus

items on his ledger sheet of miseries and comforts is that from the ship he has *"gotten out so many necessary things as will either supply my Wants, or enable me to supply my self even as long as I live."* He repeats this comfort a few paragraphs later, commenting on the "store" in his cave: "it look'd like a general Magazine of all Necessary things, and I had every thing so ready at my Hand, that it was a great Pleasure to me to see all my Goods in such Order, and especially to find my Stock of all Necessaries so great." Crusoe landed is Crusoe restored.

OPPOSITIONS

Timing is no accident in *Robinson Crusoe*. Both Defoe and his "fugitive hero" are sensitive to coincidence, Crusoe, for example, noticing that "there was a strange Concurrence of Days, in the various Providences which befel me; and which, if I had been superstitiously inclin'd to observe Days as Fatal or Fortunate, I might have had Reason to have look'd upon with a great deal of Curiosity." That Defoe sets the adventure when he does becomes yet another element of the narrative's readable potential. The politics of the island exile are live issues for Defoe: sovereignty, property, natural law, and toleration. Crusoe reinvents what the Stuarts abused, though in the instance of toleration it requires a few years worth of taxing conversation between Crusoe's self and soul on the subject of cannibalism to sort out the issues involved.

Crusoe's adventures on the island are such that they conform to the standard exigencies of exilic experience. During the earlier years on the island, he is trapped between his desire for settlement and his readiness to depart an uninhabited, strange, and lonely place. He is vaguely aware that he must organize his territory on what he comes to call "my beloved Island' so that he can both transform it as a new home and keep paramount any opportunity to leave it. To place himself any distance from the seaward part of the island, from which he could be more easily rescued if circumstance permitted, would, as he puts it, "anticipate my Bondage." But until the time is ready in the larger scheme of things that Crusoe calls Providence, he is tethered. Crusoe may plan an escape by carving a huge canoe out of a felled tree, but to his dismay he realizes that he has no way of hauling the finished craft to the sea. Poor Crusoe tries to make too much of opportunity before opportunity is ready to make something of him.

The turning point of Crusoe's stay on the island, the point at which the slow process of opportunity begins to shape the necessity for departure, is also the point at which the idea of sovereignty begins to take on different dimensions. This process begins with the famous footprint episode, during the fifteenth year of Crusoe's isolation. Crusoe himself recognizes the moment as an incursion that is also a turning or transition point in his exile: "But now I come to a new Scene in my Life." Perhaps no scene in fiction better illustrates the subtle workings of surface and depth patternings that narrative has available to it. Crusoe, wandering over now familiar territory, comes on a startling sight, the image of a single footprint in the sand. This stark impression provides his hard-won resettlement—his recessed allegorical history—its most dramatic surface test. At the appearance of the print, Crusoe's lingering despair at his separation from the world he once knew turns into an absolute and immanent fear of having his sovereignty violated, his settlement in exile penetrated. The paradox of the exilic condition is fully realized in a single narrative incident: the necessitous strength of character that allows Crusoe to re-create a version of home abroad also inhibits and distorts the exile's traditional *Drang nach Hause,* his will to return to his original place.

The footprint episode recalls Crusoe's earlier shock at the sudden greeting of his wild parrot, when the sound of another voice so rattled him that it took him "a good while before I could compose my self." But Crusoe is not so fortunate after sighting the print which, even years later, still "discompos'd me very much." He is at first thunderstruck "as if I had seen an Apparition," and his recidivistic response is to wander up and down the beach just as he had done when he set his own foot on the island nearly fifteen years before. He immediately adjusts his language to suit his material circumstances; homecoming now becomes a form of self-defense: "like a Man perfectly confus'd and out of my self, I came Home to my Fortification, not feeling, as we say, the Ground I went on." Out of himself, he is like the apparition he thinks he has just seen, but his supposed apparition has a very tangible quality to it—it makes a real impression or, at least, a footprint—whereas Crusoe is so scared his feet barely touch the ground.

The confusion here of Crusoe's self with sign—later he hopes the footprint, like the imprint of the parrot's voice, would turn out to be his own—derives from the strength of his desire that his settlement, once so separable from all he had known, now be integral as all he has left. The print in the sand is both an image of trespass on the exile's territory and a strong but necessary reminder that the exile's isolated condition is an unnatural one. Crusoe's fear initially renders him as wild as any being who might have made the print, that is, renders him too native an inhabitant—one with no civilized history other than his island life. He ran home

> terrify'd to the last Degree, looking behind me at every two or three Steps, mistaking every Bush and Tree, and fancying every Stump at a Distance to be a Man; nor is it possible to describe how many various Shapes affrighted Imagination represented Things to me in, how many wild Ideas were found every Moment in my Fancy, and what strange unaccountable Whimsies came into my Thoughts by the Way.

When Crusoe tries to soothe himself with the hope that the footprint might, after all, be his own, that hope is dashed in an appropriate externalization of internal apprehension: the print turns out to be too large. For the fearful Crusoe, the mysterious impression on the beach assumes in size a power opposite to the self-diminishment he experiences on seeing it. The print is even more threatening in its singleness: one print suggests its complement, its "other." To put its significance differently, Crusoe learns from the surface appearance of the footprint a deeper exilic lesson he ought never to have forgotten and will remember for the rest of his stay on the island: one simply cannot go it alone forever. By its singleness, which is to say its incompleteness, the one print in the sand is both a complement to Crusoe's condition and a corrective to any permanent historical notion about the possibility or desirability of the exile's lone sovereignty. By the habit of abundant years, Crusoe had already begun to cultivate permanent thoughts that ought to have remained provisional: "when I began to regret the want of Conversation, I would ask my self whether thus conversing mutually with my own Thoughts, and, as I hope I may say, with even God himself by Ejaculations, was not better than the utmost Enjoyment of humane Society in the World."

An earlier passage in which Crusoe, aware of the hyperbole, describes the nature of his supposed sovereignty suggests why the appearance of the print on the beach is so crucial a point in the narrative: "I was Lord of the whole Mannor; or if I pleas'd, I might call my self King, or Emperor over the whole Country which I had Possession of. There were no Rivals. I had no Competitor, none to dispute Sovereignty of Command with me." "Rivals," "Competitor," and "Sovereignty" are key words here, and the sighting of the footprint signals the imposition of new circumstances for Crusoe, circumstances that are, willy-nilly, political. If Defoe chose to represent Crusoe's island reign as coincidentally "occupying" the Restoration hiatus in England, he also gave considerable thought to what sort of action affects the alteration of historical circumstance. In the exilic state, rivalry is opportunity; in the usurped state, rivalry is disaster. The two possibilities conform to the status of narrative as sovereign on the one hand, sufficient unto its made-up self, and representational on the other, reflecting the contingencies and necessities of the supposed real world it imitates. This is the same point I make in the introductory chapter about the double quality of Molloy's "region," both insulated and penetrated, in the Samuel Beckett novel that serves as a modern comic analogue to the Crusoe dilemma. Fiction is threatened or, as Edward Said would put it, molested by its own compulsion to penetrate its exilic allegory with the figure of oppositional reality.

The footprint in Defoe's narrative is incontestably a sign of opposition to Crusoe—surely he reads it that way—and, given the care Defoe takes in marking its appearance in the fifteenth year of Crusoe's reign, the historically temporal parallel at "home" is intriguing. Crusoe sees the footprint in 1674, assuming he lands on the island in 1659, as he originally says, and not in 1658, as he later seems to think. Nearly every observer of the course of Stuart history pointed to a different set of circumstances after the first fifteen years of Charles II's reign. Those actively involved in the politics of the period such as Andrew Marvell, Anthony Ashley Cooper, Algernon Sidney, and John Locke, and those that were to write of it in the next generation, Laurence Echard, John Oldmixon, and Daniel Defoe, marked 1674 as a transition from the earlier monarchical consolidation of power to the emergence, within the context of plots and conspiracies, of a newly named opposition party and a new crisis in national sovereignty. In his *Growth of Popery and Arbitrary Power* (1678), Marvell wrote that after 1674 the king's new party, the Tories, tried to stir the old royalist antirevolutionary fervor against the new Whigs: "They begun therefore after fifteen years to remember that there were such a sort of men in England as the old Cavalier party; and reckoned, that by how much the more generous, they were more credulous than others, and so more fit to be again abused."

For the Stuarts, the emergence of a powerful opposition after 1674 plotted the beginning of a long road to the end; for Crusoe, the end to his unviolated hegemony during 1674 plotted the beginning of a long road to a new beginning. The potential represented by the footprint is what is required to get Crusoe back to his first home, his "real" home, the one on the map. In the oft-cited "Chequer Work of Providence" passage, Crusoe admits the absurdity of having feared as violation what he ought better to have welcomed as possible salvation.

> For I whose only Affliction was, that I seem'd banished from human Society, that I was alone, circumscrib'd by the boundless Ocean, cut off from Mankind, and condemn'd to what I call'd silent Life; that I was as one who Heaven thought not worthy to be number'd among the Living, or to appear among the rest of his Creatures; that to have seen one of my own Species, would have seem'd to me a Raising me from Death to Life, and the greatest blessing that Heaven it self, next to the supreme Blessing of Salvation, could bestow; *I say,* that I should now tremble at the very Apprehensions of seeing a Man, and was ready to sink into the Ground at but the Shadow or silent Appearance of a Man's having set his Foot in the Island.

Crusoe may be ready to recognize the irony of his initial reaction, but he is not yet prepared to alter his behavior. He has the exilic terms reversed, if his desire is historical reprise: "In my Reflections upon the State of my Case, since I came on Shore on this Island, I was comparing the happy Posture of My Affairs, in the first Years of my Habitation here, compar'd to the Life of Anxiety, Fear and Care, which I had liv'd ever since I had seen the Print of a Foot in the Sand." Someone made that print and Crusoe is unready to deem that someone savior or friend. In fact, for years he reacts to his opposition, real or presumed, as would the worst of tyrants securing the safety of his tyranny: "these Anxieties, these constant Dangers I liv'd in, and the Concern that was now upon me, put an End to all Invention, and to all the Contrivances that I had laid for my Future

Accommodations and Conveniences." In the political pattern of the action, Defoe ironically endows his governor in exile with the most oppressive features of the Stuart regime whose reign he temporally counters. In the strictly narrative pattern, Crusoe's exaggerated fears for his own security obsessively protect a "created" realm by putting an end to its invention, by ceasing to create it: "I had the Care of my Safety more now upon my Hands, than that of my Food. I car'd not to drive a Nail, or chop a Stick of Wood now, for fear the Noise I should make should be heard; much less would I fire a Gun, for the same Reason."

"At This Hour Lie at My Mercy All Mine Enemies"

It takes Crusoe several years of paranoid defensiveness to get used to the notion that what seems to be his opposition might actually be the means by which he can alter his condition as exile. The sighting of the print refocuses the exilic dilemma—that which had been appropriated as a substitute has become for Crusoe a necessity. Something has gone wrong in ways that even Crusoe comes to recognize, and in the latter years of his stay he begins the process of reconversion and recivilization. He makes positive again what his father, in overstressing security at home, had so many years before envisaged as strictly negative: "I could not satisfy my self in my Station, but was continually poring upon the Means, and Possibility of my Escape from this Place." The neutral, indeed, almost scathing "Place" tells much of the story. Like Odysseus's renewed urge for home while tethered on Calypso's island, or like Prospero's homeward turn after burying his staff on his magical isle, Crusoe reexperiences the exile's original desire: any place but home for him now is undifferentiated. Once Crusoe's counterturn is set in motion things move, if not as quickly as he would choose, at least decisively. He readies himself for actual homecoming by planning a preliminary beachhead on the cannibal mainland.

> All my Calm of Mind in my Resignation to Providence, and waiting the Issue of the Dispositions of Heaven, seem'd to be suspended; and I had, as it were, no Power to turn my Thoughts to any thing, but to the Project of a Voyage to the Main, which came upon me with such Force, and such an Impetuosity of Desire, that it was not to be resisted.

Crusoe gives up his scheme to go to the cannibal Main only when one very useful cannibal comes to him. Friday's companionship during the last few years of Crusoe's exile provides an actual other who becomes a second self in initiating the strength of will toward repatriation. Friday sees his own land from a vantage point on the high side of Crusoe's island: *"O joy! Says he, O glad! There see my Country, there my Nation!"* These stirring words are voiced just after Crusoe anticipates the spatial collapse of the distance between the place of exile and his own home island nation by referring to himself and Friday as "comforted restor'd Penitents; we had here the Word of God to read, and no farther off from his Spirit to instruct, than if we had been in *England*." The solace of one land for Friday and the mention of another by Crusoe prime the narrative for what is about to happen.

After Friday's arrival, and without precisely knowing why, Crusoe assumes his deliverance is again providentially opportune, telling of "the great Hopes I had of being effectually, and speedily deliver'd; for I Had an invincible Impression upon my Thoughts, that my Deliverance was at hand, and that I should not be another Year in this Place." The impression that the times are ready for him to return seems as telling in its way as the impression of the footprint years before. Crusoe loses his fear of having his island penetrated when he loses the desire to remain isolated.

In the interim between Crusoe's thoughts about redirecting his efforts toward home and his opportunity to make the break, he begins to revise his notions of what sovereignty ought to mean to him in historical rather than fictional terms. He turns to the law of civilized nations, and he does so by readjusting his view of those cannibals whose intermittent presence on the island had so reduced him to quivering paranoia and unaccountable bloodlust. Divine Right, Crusoe decides, ought to be in the hands of a Divinity, not in the hands of a self-appointed vice-regent. God has not called on him, Crusoe says, "to take upon me to be a Judge of their Actions, much less an Executioner of his Justice; that whenever he thought fit, he would take the Cause into his own Hands, and by national Vengeance punish them as a People, for national Crimes; but that in the mean time, it was none of my Business." Any one individual, namely Crusoe in this instance, cannot afford to be a scourge on an entire nation, and at the end of his stay, his energies are better employed against those few who have falsely usurped a power that they have no right to hold, that is, against the English mutineers who run riot in conspiracy and betrayal.

At the original sighting of the mutineers and their unfortunate captives, matters come to a head. Crusoe approaches the captives with the mutineers out of earshot and chooses to ally himself with those who face either an exile like his own or, worse, death. That is, he allies himself with historical legitimacy, with the rightful captain of the English vessel. As soon as matters indeed "right" themselves, the English usurpers and mutineers are cast out from that which they have misappropriated. Later we learn that their fate, too, becomes exilic: "they would much rather venture to stay there, than to be carry'd to *England* to be hang'd; so I left it on that Issue." The politics of Crusoe's narrative are played out in miniature by the scoundrels suffering what they would have wished upon the forces of legitimacy.

While still in dire straits, the English captain contemplates the bizarre figure of Crusoe as ally coming toward him, a bedraggled version of the mythical stranger-savior figure of legendary tales. Crusoe says to the captain: "But can you put a Stranger in the way how to help you, for you seem to me to be in some great Distress? I saw you when you landed, and when you seem'd to make Applications to the Brutes that came with you, I saw one of them lift up his Sword to kill you." The captain looks at this apparition and elevates Crusoe beyond or, as Crusoe's father would see it, higher than his merits: *"Am I talking to God, or Man! Is it a real Man, or an Angel!"* Crusoe's self-identification is significant here after twenty-eight years on the island and nearly thirty-seven years away from home: "I am a Man, an *Englishman,* and dispos'd to assist you." The island sovereign now names himself citizen of his native country, bringing his alien status and resettling impulse into alignment. Again, like Prospero, Crusoe is a magic (or imagined) island recluse willing to become a national subject once certain conditions are met, certain contracts arranged, certain powers displayed. Friday, as commentators have noticed, is Crusoe's Ariel.

> Let them be hunted soundly. At this hour
> Lie at my mercy all mine enemies.
> Shortly shall all my labors end, and thou

Shalt have the airs at freedom. For a little,
Follow, and do me service.

(Tempest, 4.1.262–66)

Crusoe's actions at the end reveal a homeward turn of mind and a set of principles based on necessity. His advice about firing on, and possibly killing, the mutineers justifies violence for legal, not tyrannical, ends: "*Necessity* legitimates my Advice." And Crusoe's forces advance in the name of rightful authority: "At the Noise of the Fire, I immediately advanc'd with my whole Army, which was now 8 Men, *viz.* my self *Generalissimo,* Friday, my Lieutenant-General, the Captain and his two Men, and the three Prisoners of War, who we had trusted with Arms." Perhaps this force is not so impressive as the advance guard of William III riding into England, but it is surely more effective than the hopeless army in which Defoe may have fought that suffered ignominious earlier defeat at Sedgemoor against the forces of James II in 1685.

Crusoe arrives back in England on June 11, 1687. He comes home truly substantiated, both in status—as returned wanderer, a man of archetypal value—and in funds from his Brazilian plantation, which Defoe totals later at "above a thousand Pounds a Year, as sure as an Estate of Lands in *England.*" Defoe's analogy exceeds even the wishes of Crusoe's father: his exile progresses metaphorically as adventurer from the merchant class to the settled gentry. Crusoe's accumulated property allows him to return, in a sense, properly islanded. Perhaps in a broader sense, Crusoe's substantial return to his native place allows Defoe to realize the full potential of an action in which the exile, abroad and restored, is always sovereign.

Man Friday

A. D. Hope

It was after this some considerable Time, that being upon the top of
the Hill, at the *East* Side of the Island, from whence as I have said, I
had in a clear Day discover'd the Main, or Continent of *America;
Friday,* the Weather being very serene, looks very earnestly towards
the Main Land, and in a kind of Surprise, falls a jumping and
dancing, and calls out to me, for I was at some Distance from him: I
asked him, what was the Matter? *O joy!* Says he, *O glad! There see
my Country, there my Nation!*
    I observ'd an extraordinary Sense of Pleasure appear'ed in his Face,
and his Eyes sparkled, and his Countenance discover'd a strange
Eagerness, as if he had a Mind to be in his own Country again.

DEFOE, The Life and Adventures of Robinson Crusoe, vol. 2

Saved at long last through Him whose power to save
Kept from the walking, as the watery grave,
Crusoe returned to England and his kind,
Proof that an unimaginative mind
And sober industry and common sense
May supplement the work of Providence.
He, no less providential, and no less
Inscrutably resolved to save and bless,
Eager to share his fortune with the weak
And faithful servants whom he taught to speak,
By all his years of exile undeterred,
Took into exile Friday and the bird.

The bird no doubt was well enough content.
She had her corn—what matter where she went?

Except when once a week he walked to church,
She had her master's shoulder as a perch,
She shared the notice of the crowds he drew
Who praised her language and her plumage too,
And like a rational female could be gay
On admiration and three meals a day.

But Friday, the dark Caribbean man,
Picture his situation if you can:
The gentle savage, taught to speak and pray,
On England's Desert Island cast away,
No godlike Crusoe issuing from his cave
Comes with his thunderstick to slay and save;
Instead from caves of stone, as thick as trees,
More dreadful than ten thousand savages,
In their strange clothes and monstrous mats of hair,
The pale-eyed English swarm to joke and stare,
With endless questions round him crowd and press
Curious to see and touch his loneliness.
Unlike his master Crusoe long before
Crawling half-drowned upon the desolate shore,
Mere ingenuity useless in his need,
No wreck supplies him biscuit, nails and seed,
No fort to build, no call to bake, to brew,
Make pots and pipkins, cobble coat and shoe,
Gather his rice and milk his goats, and rise
Daily to some absorbing enterprise.

And yet no less than Crusoe he must find
Some shelter for the solitary mind;
Some daily occupation to contrive
To warm his wits and keep the heart alive;
Protect among the cultured, if he can,
The 'noble savage' and the 'natural man'.
As Crusoe made his clothes, so he no less
Must labour to invent his nakedness
And, lest their alien customs without trace
Absorb him, tell the legends of his race
Each night aloud in the soft native tongue,
That filled his world when, bare and brown and young,
His brown, bare mother held him at her breast,

Then say his English prayers and sink to rest.
And each day waking in his English sheets,
Hearing the wagons in the cobbled streets,
The morning bells, the clatter and cries of trade,
He must recall, within their palisade,
The sleeping cabins in the tropic dawn,
The rapt, leaf-breathing silence, and the yawn
Of naked children as they wake and drowse,
The women chattering round their fires, the prows
Of wet canoes nosing the still lagoon;
At each meal, handling alien fork or spoon,
Remember the spiced mess of yam and fish
And the brown fingers meeting in the dish;
Remember too those island feasts, the sweet
Blood frenzy and taste of human meat.

Thus he piled memories against his need:
In vain! For still he found the past recede.
Try as he would, recall, relive, rehearse,
The cloudy images would still disperse,
Till, as in dreams, the island world he knew
Confounded the fantastic with the true,
While England, less unreal day by day,
The Cannibal Island, ate his past away.
But for the brooding eye, the swarthy skin,
That witnessed to the Natural Man within,
Year followed year, by inches, as they ran,
Transformed the savage to an Englishman.
Brushed, barbered, hatted, trousered and baptized,
He looked, if not completely civilized,
What came increasingly to the case:
An upper servant, conscious of his place,
Friendly but not familiar in address
And prompt to please, without obsequiousness,
Adept to dress, to shave, to carve, to pour
And skilled to open or refuse the door.
To keep on terms with housekeeper and cook,
But quell the maids and footmen with a look.
And now his master, thoughtful for his need,
Bought him a wife and gave him leave to breed.

A fine mulatto, once a lady's maid,
She thought herself superior to Trade
And, reared on a Plantation, much too good
For a low native Indian from the wood;
Yet they contrived at last to rub along
For he was strong and kind, and she was young,
And soon a father, then a family man,
Friday took root in England and began
To be well thought of in the little town,
And quoted in discussions at 'The Crown',
Whether the Funds would fall, the French would treat
Or the new ministry could hold its seat.
For though he seldom spoke, the rumour ran
The master had no secrets from his man,
And Crusoe's ventures prospered so, in short,
It was concluded he had friends at Court.

Yet as the years of exile came and went,
Though first he grew resigned and then content,
Had you observed him close, you might surprise
A stranger looking through the servant's eyes.
Some colouring of speech, some glint of pride,
Not born of hope, for hope long since had died,
Not even desire, scarce memory at last,
Preserved that stubborn vestige of the past.

It happened once that man and master made
A trip together on affairs of trade;
A ship reported foundered in the Downs
Brought them to visit several seaport towns.
At one of these, Great Yarmouth or King's Lynn,
Their business done, they baited at an inn,
And in the night were haunted by the roar
Of a wild wind and tide against the shore.
Crusoe soon slept again, but Friday lay
Awake and listening till the dawn of day.
For the first time in all his exiled years
The thunder of the ocean filled his ears;
And that tremendous voice so long unheard
Released and filled and drew him, till he stirred
And left the house and passed the town, to reach

At last the dunes and rocks and open beach:
Pale, bare and gleaming in the break of day
A sweep of new-washed sand around the bay,
And spindrift driving up the bluffs like smoke,
As the long combers reared their crests and broke.
There in the sand beside him Friday saw
A single naked footprint on the shore.
His heart stood still, for as he stared, he knew
The foot that made it never had worn shoe
And, at a glance, that no such walker could
Have been a man of European blood.
From such a footprint once he could describe
If not the owner's name, at least his tribe,
And tell his purpose as men read a face
And still his skill sufficed to know the race;
For this was such a print as long ago
He too had made and taught his eyes to know.
There could be no mistake. Awhile he stood
Staring at the grey German Ocean's flood;
And suddenly he saw those shores again
Where Orinoco pours into the main,
And, stunned with an incredible surmise,
Heard in his native tongue once more the cries
Of spirits silent now for many a day;
And all his years of exile fell away.

The sun was nearly to the height before
Crusoe arrived hallooing at the shore,
Followed the footprints to the beach and found
The clothes and shoes and thought his servant drowned.
Much grieved he sought him up and down the bay
But never guessed, when later in the day
They found the body drifting in the foam,
That Friday had been rescued and gone home.

Chronology

1660	Daniel Foe born in London to a fairly prosperous tallow chandler, James Foe, and his wife, Alice
1662	Family follows their pastor, Dr. Samuel Annesley, out of the Church of England because of the Act of Uniformity; they are now Presbyterians.
ca. 1668	Mother dies.
ca. 1671–79	Studies at the Reverend James Fischer's school at Dorking, Surrey, then, Oxford and Cambridge being closed to Dissenters, attends the Reverend Charles Morton's School at Newington Green. Foe's education, although preparing him for the ministry, includes science and is broader than studies at the universities.
1683	Merchant in the import/export business in Freeman's Yard, Cornhill (London). Publishes first political tract; no copy is known.
1684	Marries Mary Tuffley, daughter of a prosperous Dissenting wine-cooper. She bears him eight children, six of whom survive.
1685–92	Prospers in business: trades in hosiery, imports wine and tobacco, insures ships. Travels in England and on the Continent for business. Publishes political tracts.
1685	Joins the Protestant Duke of Monmouth's rebellion against Catholic James II: manages to escape after the disastrous Battle of Sedgemoor.
1688–1702	Supports William III, serving him in various offices.
1688	Admitted to the Butcher's Company, a guild. Publishes his first extant political tract against James II.

	Rides to Henley to join the advancing forces of William of Orange.
1690–91	Contributes to the *Athenian Mercury;* belongs to the Athenian Society.
1692	Declares bankruptcy, a result of rash speculations and losses in his ship insurance caused by the war with France. Within ten years, pays back all but £5,000, but is never again quite clear of debt.
1695	When manager-trustee of the royal lotteries, changes his name to "De Foe."
1697	Publishes *An Essay upon Projects,* which attracts politicians' attention.
1701	Publishes *The True-Born Englishman: A Satyr,* a poetic defense of William III's Dutch ancestry. Youngest child, Sophia, baptized.
1702	William III dies; Anne's accession ends Defoe's hopes of preferment. The rise of the Tories increases pressure on the Dissenters. Defoe writes *The Shortest Way with the Dissenters: or Proposals For The Establishment of The Church,* an ironic attack on the intolerance of the High Church.
1703	Accused of seditious libel, Defoe is arrested for writing *The Shortest Way.* Fined and sent to Newgate, sentenced to stand in the pillory. Writes *Hymn to the Pillory.* Second bankruptcy. Appeals to Harley, who secures his release and employs him. Publishes an authorized edition of his collected works.
1703–14	Pamphleteer and intelligence agent for Harley.
1704–13	Writes and edits *The Review* (a weekly, later tri-weekly), the main government organ (moderate Tory), in which Defoe discusses current affairs, politics, religion, trade, and manners and morals. The paper influences both later essay periodicals and the newspaper press.
1706–10	As government secret agent, travels frequently in Scotland to promote the Act of Union.
1708	Moves to Stoke Newington, suburb north of London, where he lives the rest of his life.
1713–14	Repeatedly arrested by Harley's political enemies,

	once for publishing ironical tracts in support of the Hanoverian succession.
1715	Publishes *The Family Instructor,* a conduct manual, his most popular didactic work.
1715–30	Undertakes propaganda and intelligence work for successive Whig ministries after Harley's fall.
1718	Publishes the second volume of *The Family Instructor.*
1719	*The Life and Strange Surprising Adventures of Robinson Crusoe of York, Mariner* and *The Farther Adventures of Robinson Crusoe.*
1720	*Memoirs of a Cavalier; The Life, Adventures, and Pyracies of the Famous Captain Singleton.*
1722	*The Fortunes and Misfortunes of the Famous Moll Flanders, A Journal of the Plague Year,* and *The History and Remarkable Life of the Truly Honourable Colonel Jacque, Commonly Call'd Colonel Jack.*
1724	*The Fortunate Mistress: Or . . . Roxana.*
1724–26	*A Tour Thro' the Whole Island of Great Britain* (three volumes).
1725	*The Complete English Tradesman* and pirate and criminal "lives."
1726	*The Political History of the Devil.*
1727	*Conjugal Lewdness* (*A Treatise Concerning the Use and Abuse of the Marriage Bed*), *An Essay on the History and Reality of Apparitions, A New Family Instructor,* and a second volume of *The Complete English Tradesman.*
1728	"Augusta Triumphans: Or, The Way To Make London The most flourishing city in the Universe" and *A Plan of the English Commerce.*
1731	Dies of a "lethargy" in Ropemaker's Alley (London), hiding from creditors. Buried in Bunhill Fields along with John Bunyan and other Puritans.

Contributors

HAROLD BLOOM, Sterling Professor of the Humanities at Yale University, is the author of *The Anxiety of Influence, Poetry and Repression,* and many other volumes of literary criticism. His forthcoming study, *Freud: Transference and Authority,* attempts a full-scale reading of all of Freud's major writings. A MacArthur Prize Fellow, he is general editor of five series of literary criticism published by Chelsea House. During 1987–88, he was appointed Charles Eliot Norton Professor of Poetry at Harvard University.

VIRGINIA WOOLF was a famous English novelist and essayist. Her critical works include *The Common Reader* and *The Moment and Other Essays.*

IAN WATT is Professor of English at Stanford University. His books include *The Rise of the Novel, Conrad in the Nineteenth Century,* and the forthcoming *Gothic and Comic: Two Variations on the Realistic Tradition.*

G. A. STARR is Professor of English at the University of California at Berkeley. His books include *Defoe and Spiritual Autobiography* and *Defoe and Casuistry.*

J. PAUL HUNTER is Dean of the College of Arts and Sciences at the University of Rochester. He is the author of *The Reluctant Pilgrim.*

LEOPOLD DAMROSCH, JR., is Professor of English at the University of Maryland, College Park, and the author of *Samuel Johnson and the Tragic Sense, Symbol and Truth in Blake's Myth,* and *God's Plot and Man's Stories.*

MICHAEL SEIDEL is Professor of English at Columbia University. His books include *Exile and the Narrative Imagination* and *The Satiric Inheritance*.

A. D. HOPE is a prominent Australian poet and critic. He is Emeritus Professor of English at the Australian National University in Canberra and the author of numerous books of poetry and criticism.

Bibliography

Allen, Walter. *The English Novel: A Short Critical History*. London: Phoenix House, 1954.

Anderson, Hans H. "The Paradox of Trade and Morality in Defoe." *Modern Philology* 39 (1941): 23–46.

Ayers, R. W. *"Robinson Crusoe:* Allusive Allegorick History." *PMLA* 82 (1967): 399–407.

Birdsall, Virginia Ogden. *Defoe's Perpetual Seekers: A Study of the Major Fiction*. Lewisburg: Bucknell University Press, 1985.

Boardman, Michael M. *Defoe and the Uses of Narrative*. New Brunswick, N.J.: Rutgers University Press, 1983.

Braudy, Leo. "Daniel Defoe and the Anxieties of Autobiography." *Genre* 6 (1973): 76–97.

Brown, Homer. "The Displaced Self in the Novels of Daniel Defoe." *ELH* 38 (1971): 562–90.

Burke, John J., Jr. "Observing the Observer in Historical Fictions by Defoe." *Philological Quarterly* 61 (1982): 13–32.

Butler, Mary. "The Effect of the Narrator's Rhetorical Uncertainty on the Fiction of *Robinson Crusoe.*" *Studies in the Novel* 15 (1983): 77–90.

Damrosch, Leopold, Jr. "Defoe as Ambiguous Impersonator." *Modern Philology* 71 (1973): 153–59.

———. *God's Plot and Man's Stories*. Chicago: University of Chicago Press, 1985.

Ellis, F. H., ed. *Twentieth Century Interpretations of* Robinson Crusoe. Englewood Cliffs, N.J.: Prentice-Hall, 1969.

Hymer, Stephen. "Robinson Crusoe and Primitive Accumulation." *Monthly Review* 23 (1971): 11–36.

James, E. Anthony. *Daniel Defoe's Many Voices: A Rhetorical Study of Prose Style and Literary Method*. Amsterdam: Editions Rodopi N. V., 1972.

Joyce, James. "Daniel Defoe." *Buffalo Studies* 1, no. 1 (1964): 7–25.

Lannert, Gustav. "An Investigation of the Language of *Robinson Crusoe.*" Uppsala, Sweden: Uppsala University, 1910.

McKeon, Michael. *The Origins of the English Novel, 1600–1740*. Baltimore: Johns Hopkins University Press, 1987.

McKillop, A. D. *Early Masters of English Fiction*. Lawrence: University of Kansas Press, 1956.

Novak, Maximillian E. *Economics and the Fiction of Daniel Defoe.* Berkeley: University of California Press (Publications in English Studies), 1962.

———. *Realism, Myth, and History in Defoe's Fiction.* Lincoln: University of Nebraska Press, 1983.

Richetti, John J. *Defoe's Narratives: Situations and Strategies.* Oxford: Clarendon, 1975.

Rogers, Pat. *Robinson Crusoe.* London: Allen & Unwin, 1979.

Spacks, Patricia Meyer. "The Soul's Imaginings: Daniel Defoe, William Cowper." *PMLA* 91 (1976): 420–35.

Starr, George A. *Defoe and Casuistry.* Princeton: Princeton University Press, 1965.

Sutherland, James R. *Daniel Defoe: A Critical Study.* New York: Houghton Mifflin, 1971.

Swados, Harvey. "*Robinson Crusoe* The Man Alone." In *Twelve Original Essays on Great English Novels,* edited by Charles Shapiro. Detroit: Wayne State University Press, 1960.

Tillyard, E. M. W. *The Epic Strain in the English Novel.* Fair Lawn, N.J.: Essential Books, 1958.

Watt, Ian. *The Rise of the Novel: Studies in Defoe, Richardson, and Fielding.* Berkeley: University of California Press, 1957.

Weinstein, Arnold. *The Fictions of the Self: 1500–1800.* Princeton: Princeton University Press, 1981.

Zimmerman, Everett. *Defoe and the Novel.* Berkeley: University of California Press, 1975.

Acknowledgments

"Robinson Crusoe" by Virginia Woolf from *Collected Essays: Volume One* by Virginia Woolf, © 1966 by Leonard Woolf. Reprinted by permission of the estate of Virginia Woolf, the Hogarth Press, and Harcourt Brace Jovanovich, Inc.

"Individualism and the Novel" (originally entitled *"Robinson Crusoe,* Individualism and the Novel") by Ian Watt from *The Rise of the Novel: Studies in Defoe, Richardson and Fielding* by Ian Watt, © 1957 by Ian Watt. Reprinted by permission of the author, the University of California Press, and Chatto & Windus Ltd.

"Crusoe and Spiritual Autobiography" (originally entitled *"Robinson Crusoe"*) by G. A. Starr from *Defoe and Spiritual Autobiography* by G. A. Starr, © 1965 by Princeton University Press. Reprinted by permission of Princeton University Press.

"Robinson Crusoe's Rebellion and Punishment" by J. Paul Hunter from *The Reluctant Pilgrim: Defoe's Emblematic Method and Quest for Form in* Robinson Crusoe by J. Paul Hunter, © 1966 by the Johns Hopkins University Press. Reprinted by permission of the Johns Hopkins University Press, Baltimore/London.

"Myth and Fiction in *Robinson Crusoe*" by Leopold Damrosch, Jr., from *God's Plot and Man's Stories* by Leopold Damrosch, Jr., © 1985 by the University of Chicago. Reprinted by permission of the University of Chicago Press.

"Crusoe's Island Exile" by Michael Seidel from *Exile and the Narrative Imagination* by Michael Seidel, © 1986 by Yale University. Reprinted by permission of Yale University Press.

"Man Friday" by A. D. Hope from *The Age of Reason* by A. D. Hope, © 1985 by A. D. Hope. Reprinted by permission of Curtis Brown (Aust.) Pty. Ltd. on behalf of the author.

Index

Division of labor, 21, 38
Don Juan (*Don Juan*), 35
Don Juan (Tellez), 34
Donne, John, 13
Don Quixote (Cervantes), 2, 34, 109
Don Quixote (*Don Quixote*), 34
Dostoevsky, Fyodor, 33
Dryden, John, 13, 29, 124
Durkheim, Emile, 38

Echard, Laurence, 128
Economic individualism: and book-
    keeping, 14–15; and capitalism,
    12–13; and the family, 17; and law
    of contract, 15; and profit motive,
    14, 17, 18; and travel, 17. *See also*
    Individualism
Eden, in *Robinson Crusoe*, 93–94, 107
Edwards, Jonathan, 86–87
Eliot, George, 34, 101
Emotion, body as affected by, 3, 10
Empiricists, and philosophy of En-
    glish, 13–14
Essay of Man (Pope), 71
Essay upon Projects, 122
Eve (*Paradise Lost*), 87
Exile, of Robinson Crusoe: versus
    home, 118–119; island as, 111–12;
    as means of transformation, 113;
    political implications of, 121–22,
    124–25, 129–30, 132

Family: Defoe's treatment of, 16–17;
    Robinson Crusoe's, 16, 119
Family Instructor, 17, 70
*Farther Adventures of Robinson Crusoe,
    The*, 16, 43, 87, 105, 119
Faust (Marlowe), 34
Faustus (*Faust*), 35
Fielding, Henry, 102
Filial disobedience. *See* Original sin
Flanders, Moll (*Moll Flanders*), 14, 17,
    44; desire for gentility of, 119–20;
    "economics of the spirit" of, 1;
    and family, 16; guilt impulse of,
    87, 109; morals of, 28; punishment
    of, 84–85
Fletcher, Giles, 90
Footprint episode: Crusoe's reaction

to, 126–27, 129; and discovery,
    60, 90; as means of altering exile,
    130; as sign of opposition, 128,
    130
Franklin, Benjamin, 98
Fraser, Simon, 57, 59
Freud, Sigmund, 1, 99, 105
Friday, 23, 35; arrival in England of,
    136–37; conversion of, 4, 70–71;
    economic role of, 62; marriage of,
    137–38; and relationship with
    Robinson Crusoe, 18, 19–20,
    63–66, 131, 132; rescue of, 4, 70;
    return to sea of, 138–39
Frye, Northrop, 107
*Further Adventures of Robinson Crusoe,
    The*, 38

Genre, theory of, 28, 29, 33
Gildon, Charles, 20, 30, 104
Glorious Revolution of *1689*, 12, 105,
    121, 122
God: Crusoe's, 4, 8, 26, 45, 130;
    Defoe's, 4, 44
Godolphin, Sidney, 5
Goldsmith, Oliver, 15–16
Gospel narratives, 28–29
Grace Abounding (Bunyan), 25
Gray, Andrew, 75
Green, T. H., on division of labor, 21,
    22
Growth of Popery and Arbitrary Power
    (Marvell), 128
Gulliver's Travels (Swift), 100
Gunn, Ben (*Treasure Island*), 82, 84

Hall, Bishop Joseph, 56
Harley, Earl of, 5, 85
Herbert, George, 71
Heroes: Defoe's, 1–2; economic motive
    of, 1–2, 14; family of, 16; morals
    of, 27–28
History of Plymouth Plantation
    (Bradford), 32
Hobbes, Thomas, 13, 93, 98
Howe, Irving, 78
Hume, David, 40, 91

tent, 75; punishment for, 76–77, 82; restlessness leading to, 71–72
Ortega, José Y Gasset, 100

Pamela (Richardson), 109
Paradise Lost (Milton), 27, 108
Parrot (of Robinson Crusoe), 21; greeting by, 40, 111–12, 126; return to Europe of, 135–36
Pascal, Blaise, 16
Patrick, Bishop, 69
Peacock, Thomas Love, 6–7
Pepys, Samuel, 25
Philosophy: of English Empiricists, 13–14; man's social nature as topic of, 40–41
Pilgrim's Progress, The (Bunyan), 2, 108; as an allegory, 81, 87; as a dream, 103
Plain Man's Pathway to Heaven (Dent), 29
Political History of the Devil, The, 88
Pomfret, John, 50
Pope, Alexander, 71, 100
Price, Martin, 1, 90
Prodigal son, Robinson Crusoe compared to, 72–74
Profit motive: and economic individualism, 14, 17, 18; and personal relationships, 20
Prospero (*The Tempest*), 130, 132
Protestantism: Ascetic, 23; conversion of Friday to, 4; desacralizing of, 87; and self as spiritual entity, 24
Proust, Marcel, 7
Providence: Defoe on, 30, 44–45; and deliverance from calamities, 49–50; and incidents at sea, 50; Robinson Crusoe on, 45, 60–61, 62–63, 64–65, 125; seventeenth-century religious literature on, 47–48
Providence books, 67
Psychology: Defoe's treatment of, 34, 88, 90; of Robinson Crusoe, 78, 91–92; of solitude, 36–37
"Pulley, The" (Herbert), 71
Punishment: island as form of, 104; of Moll Flanders, 84–85; Puritanism on, 76–77; of Robinson Crusoe, 76–77, 82

Puritanism: and Defoe, 1, 25, 31, 34, 68; and determinism, 94; and the Devil, 88; on dignity of labor, 23, 24; egalitarianism of, 27, 28; and introspection, 24–25, 80, 91–92; on man's punishment, 76–77; versus nonconformity, 83; and the novel, 33–34, 101; and Robinson Crusoe, 26, 28, 68, 81; versus secularization, 32; and solitude, 89; and view of nature, 84

Rader, Ralph, 101
Realism, 34, 100; ambiguities in, 101; circumstantial, 43; formal, 24; mimetic, 101; narrative, 43; paradoxes in, 105–6
Reasonableness of Christianity, The (Locke), 91
Regeneration, 57; gradual nature of, 59; and guidance of Friday, 64, 66; nature of, 61–62, 63
Repentance: of Robinson Crusoe, 56, 57–58, 58–60; stages in, 55–56
Reply to a Pamphlet Entitled "The Lord Haversham's Vindication of His Speech . . .," A, 39
Richardson, Samuel, 34, 79
Richetti, John, 83, 104
Ricoeur, Paul, 105
Riesman, David, 90, 91
Robert, Marthe, 106, 107
Robinson Crusoe: adult versus child version of, 101–2; allegorical implications of, 81–82, 83, 87, 90, 114, 116–18; autobiographical nature of, 25, 38, 39, 81, 102, 104; beginning of, 8; as children's book, 2, 101–2; critics on, 38, 67–68; depravity concept in, 69–70, 71; economic aspects of, 17–18, 97–99; ending of, 91; French versions of, 20–21; historical implications of, 102–3; individual's daily activities in, 24; as a masterpiece, 7; as myth of capitalism, 14–16, 36, 97–99; preface to, 38, 39, 102, psychological objections to, 36–37; and Puritan tradition, 26, 28, 68, 81; role of "timing" in, 125; scriptural allusions in,